The Woman Who
Created Frankenstein

The Woman Who Created Frankenstein

A Portrait of Mary Shelley

by Janet Harris

HARPER & ROW, PUBLISHERS
New York, Hagerstown, San Francisco, London

Chronology adapted from *Mary Shelley: The Author of Frankenstein,* by Elizabeth Nitchie. Copyright 1953 by the Trustees of Rutgers College in New Jersey. Adapted by permission of Rutgers University Press.

"Frankenstein on Film" adapted from *In Search of Frankenstein* by Radu Florescu. Copyright © 1975 by Radu Florescu. Adapted by permission of Little, Brown & Company in association with the New York Graphic Society.

The Woman Who Created Frankenstein: A Portrait of Mary Shelley
Copyright © 1979 by Janet Harris

FIRST EDITION

Library of Congress Cataloging in Publication Data
Harris, Janet.
    The woman who created Frankenstein.

    Bibliography: p.
    Includes index.
    SUMMARY: A biography of the 19th-century woman who
wrote the first work of science fiction.
    1. Shelley, Mary Wollstonecraft Godwin, 1797–1851—
Biography—Juvenile literature.   2. Authors, English—
19th century—Biography.   3. Shelley, Mary Wollstone-
craft Godwin, 1797–1851. Frankenstein.   [1. Shelley,
Mary Wollstonecraft Godwin, 1797–1851.   2. Authors,
English]   I. Title.
PR5398.H3   823'7 [B] [92]   78-19481
ISBN 0-06-022228-X
ISBN 0-06-022229-8 lib. bdg.

For Paul Piatti,
Friend of my heart.

Acknowledgments

I should like to thank the trustees of the MacDowell Colony for the fellowship that enabled me to begin this book, and the trustees and William Smart of the Virginia Center for the Creative Arts, where most of it was written.

Contents

The Woman Who
Created Frankenstein

1

"I Saw the Hideous Phantasm"

It was a perfect night for ghost stories.

Outside the stone-fronted mansion that was called Villa Diodati a cold wind roared, echoed in the valleys of the towering Swiss Alps, bringing rain that splashed in spurts against the shuttered windows and poured in sheets from the high gables.

It was the sort of night that eighteen-year-old Mary Godwin—now sitting half-hidden in the firelight, removed a little from the three men in whose company she felt shy—had described in a letter a month earlier:

The thunderstorms that visit us are grander and more terrific than I have ever seen before. . . . One night, the lake was lit up, the pines on Jura made visible, and all the scene illuminated for an in-

3

stant, when a pitchy blackness succeeded, and the thunder came in frightful bursts over our heads amid the darkness.

The whole summer of 1816 was like that—a summer "more like a winter." It was the coldest on record throughout the entire Northern hemisphere. Astrologers, seeing mysterious patches on the sun in their telescopes, had announced the end of the world for the middle of June. Meteorologists of the time took a more scientific approach. They attributed the eerie cold to a great increase in atmospheric dust following a volcanic explosion in the East Indies the previous year. The rains, constant and incessant, took their toll as the summer wore on. The Arve and Rhone rivers overflowed their banks, flooding the nearby Swiss cities. Bridges were washed away, roads became impassable, and Lake Geneva had risen by almost seven feet.

Not that Mary herself minded the weather. In a way, the climate outside matched her inner storms. Here she was, the mother of an infant branded by the tight morality of the day with the stigma of illegitimacy. Percy Bysshe Shelley, the baby's father, with whom she had run away two years earlier when she was only sixteen, was a fugitive from "decent society." Together they had scandalized England. Shelley was a brilliant young poet, the rebellious son of a rich and titled family. At eighteen he had been expelled from Oxford for writing an atheistic tract; at nineteen he had married, against her family's wishes, a beautiful sixteen-year-old named Harriet Westbrook. Two years later he had left Harriet, the mother of one baby and expecting another, to elope with Mary Wollstonecraft Godwin, the daughter of William Godwin, the famous radical philosopher, an opponent of kings and government, and Mary Wollstonecraft, the controversial writer who had dared to tell women they were equal to men.

Even more shocking to the British nobility and country were Mary and Shelley's companions. The young couple and their baby had taken a cottage called Chapuis, near the Villa Diodati, to be close to Lord Byron, the best-known poet and perhaps the most feared and hated man in England.

George Gordon, Lord Byron, had achieved both popular and critical acclaim at the age of twenty-four with the publication of the first two cantos of *Childe Harold's Pilgrimage* in 1812. As he himself explained, "I awoke one morning and found myself famous." But a series of scandalous love affairs—including a shadowy relationship with his half-sister, Augusta, and a much publicized separation from his wife—had turned Byron from society's spoiled darling to its scapegoat. This stay in Switzerland was the first season of his permanent self-exile from England.

Byron at twenty-eight was a figure calculated to break the heart of every woman he met. He was tall, handsome, with flowing dark hair and the profile of a young Greek god; heavy-lidded, long-lashed dark eyes; a full, sensual mouth. His love affairs and his reputation as a heartbreaker had fascinated Claire Clairmont, Mary's stepsister. Six months earlier she had seduced him. Although Byron was already tired of

5

lovesick Claire, she had somehow arranged for this summer together with Mary and Shelley and a friend of Byron's, Dr. John Polidori, by tempting Byron with the prospect of meeting Shelley, whose work she knew the handsome adventurer admired.

Slender, gray-eyed Mary, with her reserved manners and her quiet voice, felt odd man out in this vivid company. She and Shelley were deeply in love. She knew he not only adored her but respected her mind too, for Shelley was incapable of any other kind of love for a woman. Had he not written that he was lost in admiration for her "subtle and exquisitely fashioned intelligence . . . a spirit that sees into the truth of things, free from vulgar superstition"? Alone with Shelley or her family, Mary was sure of herself—her father even had described her as "imperious"—but in this glittering company she felt inadeqate, and she fought against pulling into a protective shell.

Even Claire made Mary feel dull, plain, unattractive. Claire was a lazy beauty. She had inherited dusky skin, black hair, a sultry glow. And Claire had other qualities too. She was vivacious, charming—a little crazy, Mary thought, but in a way that entranced men. She and Shelley were close—Mary sometimes thought too close. Claire appealed to a part of Shelley that Mary could not: his wild, occult imagination. Mary often would think about one episode, in particular, that Shelley had described in the journal he and Mary kept:

"Friday, October 7 [1815]," the journal reads:

Mary goes to bed at half-past eight; Shelley sits up

6

with Claire.* At 1 o'clock Shelley observes that it is the witching time of night; he inquires soon after if it is not horrible to feel the silence of night tingling in our ears; . . . at two they retire awestruck and hardly daring to breathe. Shelley says to Claire "Good night"; his hand is leaning on the table; he is conscious of an expression in his countenance which he cannot repress. Claire hesitates. "Good night" again. She still hesitates. "Did you ever read the tragedy of Orra?" said Shelley. "Yes—How horribly you look—take your eyes off." "Good night" again, and Claire ran to her room. Shelley, unable to sleep, kissed Mary and prepared to sit beside her & read until morning, when rapid footsteps descended the stairs. Claire was there; her countenance was distorted most unnaturally by horrible dismay—it beamed with a whiteness that seemed almost like light; her lips and cheeks were of one deadly hue; . . . her hair came prominent and erect; her eyes were wide and staring . . . and the eyeballs, without any relief, seemed as if they had been newly inserted, in ghastly sport, in the sockets of a lifeless head. This frightful spectacle endured but for a few moments—it was displaced by terror and confusion, violent, indeed, and full of dismay, but human. She asked me (Shelley) if I had touched her pillow (her tone was that of dreadful alarm). I said, "No, no!" . . . She told me that a pillow

---

*Claire's name was originally Jane, and she changed it later. In the interests of clarity I have quoted her as Claire throughout, even though Mary's diary reflects whichever of her names is current. (I have also taken the liberty of Americanizing the punctuation in Mary's diary entries.)

placed upon her bed had been removed, in the moment that she turned her eyes away to a chair at some distance, and evidently by no human power. . . . Her manner convinced me that she was not deceived. We continued to sit by the fire, at intervals engaging in awful conversation relative to the nature of these mysteries. . . . Just as dawn was struggling with moonlight, Claire remarked in me that unutterable expression which had affected her with so much horror before; she described it as expressing a mixture of deep sadness and conscious power over her. I covered my face with my hands, and spoke to her in the most studied gentleness. It was ineffectual; her horror and agony increased even to the most dreadful convulsions. She shrieked and writhed on the floor. I ran to Mary; I communicated in a few words the state of Claire. I brought her to Mary. The convulsions gradually ceased, and she slept. At daybreak we examined her apartment and found her pillow on the chair.

It was not only Claire, but indeed all of the party except Mary herself whose hypnotic hysteria appealed to Shelley's love of the fantastic. John William Polidori, a strange young man who was more often than not the butt of Byron's sardonic jokes, was also fascinated by occult sciences. And here, tonight, was Byron himself talking endlessly about the powers that lie beyond the conscious—unheard and unseen by the naked eye, the haunts and ghosts of a semiworld.

Byron had begun the conversation. Seated comfortably before the huge fireplace, speaking in a voice that rose above the sounds of the storm on this June night, he began to read aloud from a book that he had purchased from a Genevan bookdealer. It was titled *Fantasmagoriana*, a collection of the "Histories of Apparitions, Spectres, Ghosts, etc." The tale Byron chose was the story of a husband who kissed his new bride on their wedding night only to find, to his horror, that she had been transformed into the corpse of the woman he had once loved. Then, to heighten the horror that the story produced, Byron recited in dramatic tones lines from a then unpublished poem, Samuel Taylor Coleridge's "Christabel":

> Then drawing in her breath aloud
> Like one that shuddered, she unbound
> The cincture from beneath her breast;
> Her silken robe and inner vest
> Dropt to her feet, and full in view
> Behold! her bosom and half her side—
> A sight to dream of, not to tell!
> O shield her! shield sweet Christabel!

The voice grew silent, and for a few moments the company sat quietly, immersed in the sounds of the storm. Lightning flashed, the room brightened and then again plunged into semidarkness, as the candles flickered. The combination of the natural phenomenon and the mood left by the horror story prompted Byron to relate how he had seen a tree "spun into life by lightning."

Could lightning—the energy of the universe condensed into naked power zigzagging across the heavens—actually animate life? Mary heard her own quiet

9

voice mention the name of Dr. Erasmus Darwin, who was said to have recently conducted an experiment in which he preserved a piece of narrow spaghetti in glass "till by some extraordinary means it began to move"! The idea stirred the group's imagination. Perhaps the token parts of a creature might be put together and shocked into vital warmth—into life itself!

Throughout the conversation, Mary's eyes were on Shelley. She watched him growing paler. His imagination was clearly taking over again, she thought. Suddenly, Shelley shrieked, put his hands to his head, and ran out of the room. Polidori swiftly followed him and gave him the sedative used at the time—a whiff of ether from a flask he had on hand for such emergencies.

By the time Shelley's hallucination was over, the storm had ended and the first clear light of morning was beginning to seep through the shutters, across the polished parquet floor. Byron, unwilling to end the evening, had a suggestion. "We will each write a ghost story," he directed as Mary and Shelley, now spent and quiet after his vision, prepared to go back to their own cottage.

Shelley's burst of terror voided his creativity for the next few days. He began, halfheartedly, to work on his "Fragment of a Ghost Story"—in which a grandmother sees a ghost made of ashes—intended for his son, William. Byron, too, set to work on a fragment piece, "The Vampire," which was later appended to a major poem, *Mazeppa*. Polidori, according to Mary, wrote a story about a skull-headed lady who was punished for peeping through a keyhole. "All have begun their ghost stories," Mary wrote, "except for me."

Byron's assignment continued to haunt Mary. If only, she wrote, she could think of

a story to rival those which had excited us to this task. One which would speak to the mysterious fears of our nature and awaken thrilling horror— one to make the reader dread to look around, to curdle the blood and quicken the beatings of the heart. If I did not accomplish these things, my ghost story would be unworthy of its name. I thought and pondered—vainly. I felt that blank incapability of invention which is the greatest misery of authorship.

But much more important was her need to please Shelley. "Have you thought of a story?" she was asked each morning, and Mary, feeling more than ever inadequate, writes, "I was forced to reply with a mortifying negative."

The preoccupation continued all through the day and well into the next few nights. Then, finally, unbidden and unexpectedly, after still another night at Villa Diodati in which Dr. Darwin's experiment once again was the topic of the evening, the vision appeared. Here is the story in Mary's own words:

Night waned upon this talk, and even the witching hour had gone by before we retired to rest. When I placed my head on the pillow, I did not sleep, nor could I be said to think. My imagination, unbidden, possessed and guided me, gifting the successive images that arose in my mind with a vividness far beyond the usual bounds of reverie. I saw—with shut eyes, but acute mental vision—I saw the pale student of unhallowed arts kneeling beside the thing he had put together. I saw the hideous phantasm of a man stretched out, and then, on the working of some powerful engine show signs of life and stir with an uneasy, half-vital motion. Frightful it must be; for supremely frightful would be the effect of any human endeavor to mock the stupendous mechanism of the Creator of the world. His success would terrify the artist; he would rush away from his odious handiwork, horror-stricken. He would hope that, left to itself, the slight spark of life which he had communicated would fade, that this thing, which had received such imperfect animation, would subside into dead matter, and he might sleep in the belief that the silence of the grave would quench forever the transient existence of the hideous corpse which he had looked upon as the cradle of life. He sleeps; but he is awakened; he opens his eyes; behold, the horrid thing stands at his bedside, opening his curtains and looking on him with yellow, watery, but speculative eyes.

I opened mine in terror. The idea so possessed my mind that a thrill of fear ran through me, and I wished to exchange the ghastly image of my fancy for the realities around. I see them still: the very room, the dark parquet, the closed shutters with the moonlight struggling through, and the sense I had that the glassy lake and white high Alps were beyond. I could not so easily get rid of my hideous phantom; still it haunted me. I must try to think of something else. I recurred to my ghost story—my tiresome, unlucky ghost story! Oh! If I could only contrive one which would frighten my reader as I myself had been frightened that night!

Swift as light and as cheering was the idea that broke in upon me. "I have found it! What terrified me will terrify others; and I need only describe the spectre which had haunted my midnight pillow." On the morrow I announced that I had *thought of a story.* I began that day with the words, "It was on a dreary night of November," making only a transcript of the grim terrors of my waking dream.

Frankenstein was born!

2

A Matchless Union

"Methinks it is a wonderful work for a girl of 19—not nineteen, indeed at that time," Byron wrote to John Murray, a publisher, not too long after *Frankenstein* appeared. It was, in truth, a wonderful book for anyone to have written, but the fact that it was the work of a young woman still in her teens made it all the more remarkable.

The first edition of *Frankenstein* was published anonymously in 1818. By the time it was republished in 1831, it had become a minor classic, and its authorship had raised so many questions that, as Mary wrote in the new introduction,

the publishers . . . expressed a wish that I should furnish them with some account of the origin of the story . . . I shall thus give a general answer to

the question so frequently asked me—how I, then
a young girl, came to think of and to dilate upon
so hideous an idea. . . .

"It is not singular that, as the daughter of two persons of distinguished literary celebrity," Mary continues, "I should very early in life have thought of
writing." Indeed, so much was expected of Mary that
even as an infant she was hailed as a potential celebrity. "The only offspring of a union that will certainly
be matchless in the present generation," was the way
a popular magazine described Mary's birth on August
20, 1797. Her parents were two of England's most
glittering intellectuals, William Godwin, among England's most influential philosophers, and Mary Wollstonecraft, the founder and first spokeswoman for
feminism.

Mary had every blessing at birth—beauty, intelligence, talent, family. She was an exquisite baby. Her
milky blue eyes, fringed by long dark lashes, were to
darken as she grew older, finally becoming a subtle
blend of gray and hazel. Her flaxen ringlets, too,
would darken with the years to an arresting shade
between ash and honey. But her translucent white
skin kept its pearly sheen all her life. In an era when
fair skin was treasured in a woman, poets would write
of her "alabaster shoulders" above her "crimson evening gown," and of her swanlike throat.

Beauty was only the beginning. When Mary was
three weeks old her serious-minded father brought in
a neighbor skilled in phrenology—the then-popular
science of analyzing personality and ability by the
"bumps" of the skull. Mr. Nicholson ran his fingers

over the baby's downy little head. Then he gave his report: Mary, he thought, had "considerable memory and intelligence" and "quick sensibility." Although she might be irritable (a note in the report hints that the baby was crying), she was "surely not given to rage." Most prophetic was this announcement: Mary had "powers" that would lead to "speedy combination"—the blending of an intuitive, poetic talent and her father's legacy, a cool, clear, logical mind.

The fire certainly came from her mother. The woman who had borne Mary was the most outstanding woman of her time. The first Mary was thirty-eight when her second daughter—who was named after her—was born. In those less than four decades she crammed enough experience, excitement, achievement, for many lifetimes, and her legacy marked not only her own offspring but generations of women from her day until ours.

According to her own account, nobody rejoiced much at Mary Wollstonecraft's birth, nor was anyone particularly interested in her as a little girl. She was born on April 27, 1759, in Spitalsfield, one of the drearier sections of London. England was then in the throes of transition. The old, agrarian economy, in which people lived off the soil, was coming to an end. The country was becoming industrialized. The development of power-driven machinery brought throngs to the cities to work in huge, impersonal factories. Throughout the eighteenth century, London drew more and more people from small villages. The dark alleys and dank courtyards were filled with the immigrant poor. Silk weavers crowded families into tiny, meanly built row houses where each room hummed with the activity of men, women, and children working for pitiful wages on "piecework" to be delivered to "masters" who contracted for orders of goods.

Mary Wollstonecraft's grandfather, Edward Wollstonecraft, was one of these early capitalists. A shrewd man, his beginnings are obscure, but his hard work and business sense enabled him to describe himself as a "gentleman"—meaning a man of property—in the deed to a house he built in 1756. Far less enterprising was his only son who lived to maturity, Edward John, Mary's father. Edward John hated his trade—handkerchief weaving—and London. Nor was the wife he married while he was still an apprentice, a pretty young Irishwoman named Elizabeth, likely to fire his ambition. She was a passive, indolent person who immediately settled into what was then considered woman's lot: a steady succession of pregnancies, miscarriages, and infant deaths.

Mary's father had the "Wollstonecraft disposition": He was short-tempered, prone to fits of black despair. Yearning for love and approval, his wife made a pet of her first-born son, Ned, two years older than Mary. Mary was a toddler when another boy was born, but the baby's early death turned more adoration toward Ned and even less notice toward the little girls who followed: Eliza, born in 1764, and Everina. Eventually there were six little Wollstonecrafts, but Ned never lost his favored position in the family. Mary's resentment toward him was not helped by the terms of her grandfather's will. One third of his substantial estate was left to a daughter by an earlier marriage, one third to Mary's irresponsible father, and one third to seven-year-old Ned. Not so much as a "silver spoon apiece" went to the little girls!

Mary lived under Ned's shadow. The little boy was sent to a day school with a good library, while the little girls were reared to be docile, vain, domestic, in preparation for a "good" marriage. Ned was not the only blight on a childhood that Mary later described as a nightmare. Mary's father had the tastes of a country squire. He loved horses and the bottle, but was incompetent as a farmer. The death of Mary's grandfather freed the family from London, but her father's dream of the good life, first in rural Barking and then Yorkshire, deteriorated in drunken rages and extravagant spending sprees. Mary, the oldest daughter, became the protector of her family, often sleeping on landings to await her father's return from the tavern in order to shield her mother and the younger children from her father's furies. All her early years were spent learning to hate her father and pity her mother.

Just as Mary's family was a source of frustration to her, so was she to them. Her sisters made friends; Mary preferred her own company, fantasies in which she "talked to angels," dramatic exchanges with imaginary playmates in which she was the heroine. She yearned to right the wrongs of the world; she loathed cruelty to animals and the helpless. She flatly refused to be a "little lady." Mary's sisters were pretty, soft-spoken. Mary had a tart tongue, the corners of her mouth turned down, her eyes bulged. In an era when girls were put into stays that confined their bodies from breasts to thighs and waited anxiously for the time they could "put up their hair," Mary avoided all frivolity. In her diaries and letters there is not a single mention of a cap, gown, or bit of lace.

But if Mary's home was a torment to her, there was salvation outside. Her first friend, Jane Arden, was the daughter of a self-described "philosopher"—a man who devoted himself to the life of the mind. Mary envied Jane, who was taught literature, languages, and even math and science by her father, while her own father had nothing but scorn for "female education." Mary took to spending long hours at the Ardens', and became fiercely possessive of Jane's attention. "I am a little singular in my thoughts of love and friendship," she wrote to Jane, after a fiery quarrel. "I must have first place or none." Most young girls of the time were taught to conceal emotions, according to Claire Tomalin, her biographer, "but Mary could never wear a mask or keep a weapon in reserve."

While her friendship with Jane was both a treasure and a trial to her, everything went from bad to worse at the Wollstonecrafts'. In 1774, when Mary was fifteen, her father's desperate financial situation forced a move again, this time to Hoxton in London. Ned was apprenticed—or "articled"—to a lawyer and came home weekends to throw his weight around, "taking particular pleasure in torturing and humbling me," Mary wrote later in *Mary*, a posthumously published novel. Once again Mary found salvation outside. A family called the Clares took her under their wing, introduced her to Shakespeare and Milton and, most important, to a young protegée of theirs, Fanny Blood, who became her dearest friend.

Fanny was a little older than Mary—eighteen to Mary's sixteen—but Mary was the instigator of the friendship and by far the stronger of the two. Like her, Fanny was the eldest daughter, bright, sensitive, superior to her circumstances. She, too, had a reckless and drunken father and a gentle and spiritless mother, and the responsibility for a brood of younger children fell on Fanny's shoulders. To Mary, her friend was a mirror image. Who else but Fanny could understand all of Mary's problems, who better could share her tears and her dreams?

Fanny's empathy lent strength to Mary's growing conviction that she must strike out on her own. The future planned for her by her parents and sanctioned by her society—that of a docile wife and mother, raised to seek the protection of a husband—was a snare she must avoid. Her limited education and the lack of vocational opportunities of the time made her fit for only domestic occupations. Young women of Mary's station could become governesses or companions. Mary chose the latter. She took a position with a Mrs. Dawson, a widowed lady. The job gave her little scope for her energy and imagination, but it had its advantages. "It is a happy thing to be a mere blank," she wrote to Jane Arden, "and to be able to pursue one's own whims where they lead, without having a husband and half a hundred children to teaze [sic] and controul [sic] a poor woman who wishes to be free."

Mary's freedom—such as it was in a position in which she was little more than a servant—did not last long. She was called back to nurse her dying mother. Keeping her vigil at her mother's bedside, Mary reflected about her perceptions of woman's role. Her mother was typical of her time, and her existence had been, to Mary, a tragic one. With neither the education nor the intellectual interests to sustain her as she grew older, tyrannized by her husband, taken for granted by her children, she simply sickened and finally passed away. Her death was marked by the same kind of resignation that she had shown in life: "A little patience and all will be over" were her last words. Never, Mary resolved, would she herself be such a martyr to convention!

But despite Mary's resolution, she was still tied to her family, bound toward the protection of the younger children. She went to live with the Bloods, but her sister Everina's unhappy marriage and nervous breakdown required her to be under Mary's care. Mary's attempts to make herself, her sisters, and Fanny Blood financially independent by establishing a school for girls failed, and then another tragedy struck. Fanny left for Lisbon to marry in February of 1785; in November Mary followed her, only to find her best friend dying in childbirth. Again and again the burden of the improvident Bloods and the helpless Wollstonecrafts fell upon Mary. Duty's daughter to the end of her life, she always somehow came through, stinting on her own needs, taking work where she could find it, as a governess, a companion, and eventually a translator and writer.

Mary's first venture into writing was the result of a meeting with a remarkable man, a radical intellectual named Dr. Richard Price, whose fame had spread beyond the confines of his village, Newington Green, the site of Mary's short-lived school. American independence was then eight years old, the French Revolution was brewing, and Dr. Price's famous lecture in the Old Jewry hall in London had launched the radical English movement that supported the revolutionary ideas. Price corresponded with the most eminent scientists, writers, and revolutionists of the day in England, France, and America—men such as America's Benjamin Franklin and Thomas Jefferson, and France's Marie Jean Condorcet. More important to Mary, he gathered about him the first *women* intellectuals Mary had ever met: Ann Jebb, a political writer, and Anna Barbauld, a poet and educator. Most important of all, he swiftly recognized Mary's brilliance and courage!

Mary glowed under Dr. Price's encouragement. Inspired and stimulated by the people she met, the ideas they exchanged, she wrote her first book, a little tract based on her brief educational experiment: *Thoughts on the Education of Daughters*.

Thoughts on the Education of Daughters, tentative and often hedging, was in seed an outline of Mary's mature body of work. While she took a puritanical view of cosmetics, hair powder, card playing, and the theater, she was forthright in her contempt for women's vocational lot. For men, Mary wrote, "if they have a tolerable understanding, it has a chance to be cultivated." Not so with women. "Few are the modes of earning a subsistence, and those very humiliating." She listed the occupations: companion, schoolteacher, governess, and a few trades which were "gradually falling into the hands of men, and are certainly not very respectable"—hairdressing, millinery, midwifery, and dentistry. None of these paid well; worse, Mary wrote, there was no guarantee when women grew old unless "perhaps on some extraordinary occasion, some small allowance may be made for them, which is thought a great charity."

While Mary was putting voice to her own developing ideas about women, in France, Condorcet, the brilliant revolutionist—later to be executed by the reactionary forces that ultimately betrayed the French revolution—went much further. Linking the cause of women to the ideas of the revolution—liberty, equality, and brotherhood—Condorcet made a case for female suffrage in his *Lettres d'un Bourgeois de Newhaven à un Citoyen du Virginie*. The revolution, Condorcet thought, had already laid the foundation for the elimination of inequality. Negro slavery would end, monopolies would be abolished, a national system of insurance would abolish poverty, universal education would break down barriers of class, the beginnings of science meant that everyone would be educated. Most of all, giving women full citizenship, including the vote, would "remove the abuse of force, raise not only the status of women, but increase family happiness and reform morals." Condorcet visualized a world without tyranny, war, hunger, ignorance—and central to all this was the liberation of women!

It was heady stuff to Mary. A radical publisher named Joseph Johnson had taken her first book. He now gave her a job on his newly founded magazine, *Analytical Review*. Working at high speed, Mary turned out the first of her novels, *Maria*, and another book, *Original Stories*. But although she was developing as a writer, she was marking time while her own ideas about the rapidly changing world in which she lived—and woman's place in it—were taking form.

The spark that kindled Mary's revolutionary

ideas—and, indeed, plunged the Western world into the "Age of the Common Man"—was not long in coming. On July 14, 1789, the revolutionary forces in France stormed the Bastille. Lafayette, who led the action, turned the keys of the ancient prison over to the revolutionary who had breathed life into American independence, Thomas Paine. Across the narrow channel in England, statesmen, theorists, revolutionists, and reactionaries swiftly began to choose sides.

The forces of radical change lined up behind Mary's friend Dr. Price, while those of conservatism supported Edmund Burke. For Mary the issues were clear-cut. She rushed into print her answer to Burke's *Reflections on the Revolution in France*—a little tract fervently supporting the French Revolution, which she called *A Vindication of the Rights of Man*. Within a year she took the next step. If *men* had inalienable rights to life, liberty, and happiness, if they were not obliged to serve masters and monarchs—what about *women*? Mary took up her pen, this time to write the paper that would launch the feminist movement and make her own name a household world: *A Vindication of the Rights of Woman*.

All of Mary's anger at her second-class status as a woman, her bleak childhood, and her day-to-day struggle to find a place for herself in the intellectual world and make an independent living, went into that hastily written, fiery little pamphlet. What Mary wanted for women was that they be taken seriously. Women, she wrote, did not exist only to please men. They, like men, must "bow to the authority of reason, instead of being the *modest* slaves of opinion." Indeed, women were *equal* to men, and therefore should be subject to exactly the same political and personal treatment as men. As for their rights—these included the *right to the same education as men; the right to be governed by the same moral standards; the same political rights and obligations; and the same work opportunities.*

The pamphlet created an instant furor. Afire with her new ideas, Mary went to France in 1792 to see for herself the birth of freedom. In the bloody streets of revolution-torn Paris, Mary's life was often in danger. Even more at risk was her brave heart.

Mary was now thirty-four, no longer the plain, angry-looking young woman, but now in the full flush of her beauty. She had never been in love, and when that year it happened, it was with a passion that she, least of all, expected!

The man Mary chose to love was a romantic cad. Gilbert Imlay was an American adventurer, handsome, charming, and born to break the heart of a woman like the vulnerable intellectual he now had under his spell. Mary, whose revolutionary ideas also included free love, almost immediately became his mistress, slave, and financial support. When he tired of her as a lover—Mary had quickly become pregnant and demanded the care and consideration that her condition required—he set her to work raising money for his imaginary "businesses." All the while, Imlay was blatantly unfaithful to her. Mary tried time and time again to win him back, but it all came to nothing. She discovered that even while they were living as man and wife he was having an affair with another woman. Heartbroken, Mary sailed for England to complete her tragic plan for herself—to end her own life.

But luck, so long indifferent to Mary, suddenly took a turn. A boatman pulled her, semiconscious, out of the Putney River and revived her. Back on shore, Mary came to her senses. The foiled suicide was a cathartic for the doomed passion that for over two years had wasted her. She settled in London with her baby, who was named after the dearest friend she still mourned, Fanny Blood, and resumed her life.

Once fortune had smiled on her, it continued. Mary entered into the happiest period of her life. A few years earlier at a party given by her publisher, she had met a brilliant and famous philosopher named William Godwin. Nothing much had come of the introduction—in fact, Godwin wrote in his diary that he was unimpressed with Mary Wollstonecraft, for she talked too much, and promptly forgot her. But this time the fates were right.

The man Mary Wollstonecraft met again at the home of Mary Hays, a mutual friend, was far more famous than she. While Mary Wollstonecraft's name has been kept alive by generations of feminists, and others in her circle, Thomas Paine for example, continue to be revered, William Godwin is now nearly forgotten. Yet he was a more powerful intellect, and in his day a far greater influence, than either. Along with Rousseau and Voltaire, he was a pioneer of philosophical radicalism, a mighty fighter for the cause of individualism. Even today he would be considered a man ahead of his time.

If nothing much was expected of Mary Wollstonecraft when she was a little girl, William Godwin seemed destined for fame from childhood. An unusually precocious little boy, he was pious, studious, and greedy for distinction and praise. William was born in 1756 at Wisbech, near Cambridge, the son and grandson of Independent ministers. His home was devoted to a hellfire-and-damnation kind of religion, and William was brought up strictly in an atmosphere of self-discipline and self-examination. To train his mind he was given such gloomy reading as *An Account of the Pious Death of Many Godly Children.* Once, on a Sunday, he picked up a stray cat and hugged it in his arms. William was severely scolded for introducing a light note into the solemn Sabbath!

By the time William was eight, he had read all through the Bible. As a child his favorite pastime was preaching sermons on Sunday afternoons to the servants in the kitchen. At seventeen, destined for his father's and grandfather's profession, he became a student at the Theological College at Hoxton. He left college as he had entered it: a conservative in politics, a believer in the authority of Kings and the State, and a super-Calvinist in religion.

If Godwin had been brought up in a less rigid religion, he might not have needed to go so far in his rebellion. But as it was, his dogmatic creed began to crumble during his early experiences as a dissenting minister in country towns. He began to view the Calvinist God he had been taught to revere as a cruel tyrant, damning the innocent to eternal hell, and the government he had never questioned as keeping the workingman and the poor in subjugation to the forces of power, protecting established wealth and power.

But the most revolutionary of Godwin's ideas were his thoughts about the family. *Godwin firmly opposed marriage.* It was slavery, he wrote. No two people who live together ever completely agree. Nobody is always kind and cheerful. To get along, either husbands or wives—or at times both—had to give up their own free will. Besides, a family made one selfish, for it meant that a man considered his wife his property, and she became more important to him than the general welfare of humanity. A child needn't know its father, Godwin thought. Men and women should love freely, but not marry, and to help mothers care for children, there was always the spontaneous help of neighbors!

Godwin's ideas made him an oracle. Two of his books, *An Enquiry Concerning Political Justice*, instrumental in ending corporal punishment and directly responsible for developing the modern prison system, and *The Adventures of Caleb Williams*, a novel about injustice and oppression, made him famous. But he lived according to his ideals. A quiet, slow-spoken man with a cool, clear gaze and a high intellectual forehead, he was respected and loved by his friends, but apparently above romantic love. He lived alone in a little house cluttered with books and papers. He rose early, read Greek and Latin classics before breakfast, wrote in the afternoon, debated with his friends in the evening. Godwin had never held a woman in his arms, written a love letter, daydreamed about romance. At forty, Godwin had never been in love!

All that changed in a matter of a couple of weeks. Perhaps Godwin was forewarned: He had just read Mary Wollstonecraft's new book, *Letters Written During a Short Residence in Sweden, Norway, and Denmark*, and his emotions, so long put in cold storage, had been strangely stirred. It was, he later confessed to Mary, a book "calculated to make a man love its author."

Neither Mary nor Godwin had much to say to each other during their first real evening together at Mary Hays' house in January of 1796. But Godwin fascinated the passionate, red-haired author. She returned from a brief vacation to Berkshire in March and, "longing for some rational conversation," impulsively dropped in to visit Godwin one afternoon.

Mary, whose little house nearby was a happy, lively place, noisy with the sounds of baby Fanny's giggling and romping, made cheerful with bright curtains and pillows and warmed by a fire in the hearth, thought Godwin's a gloomy place. Godwin himself was dressed in his somber Calvinist clothes, steel-rimmed glasses perched on his ample nose. But after a moment, Godwin regained his composure at seeing his pretty neighbor on his doorstep, and invited her into his library for a pot of tea and some literary talk.

To love Godwin, Mary had to cast off her lingering passion for Imlay. It was easier than she thought. She was already seeing Godwin, and by the time she accidentally ran into Imlay romantically riding a horse in the park, she knew that the ill-fated love affair was over. She was free, finally, to care for somebody else!

The romance of this unlikely couple—Mary, a revolutionist and an intense, romantic woman, and Godwin, courageous in his thinking but cautious with his heart—should have proceeded slowly. Instead, it flowered immediately. Godwin, whose life had been lonely, had only recently, because of his new literary success, found that he was attractive to women. Now he had met the woman he didn't even know he was waiting for—one whose mind he would admire and whom he desired as well.

Not that Godwin was an intrepid lover. On July 21, he wrote Mary a tentative note: Should he write her a love letter? he asks. Her company infinitely delights him. He loves her imagination. He is charmed by the "malicious leer" in her eye. Mary flirts back; she worries that Godwin is courting two of her rivals, plump, pretty, young Amelia Alderson and an aristocratic-looking novelist named Elizabeth Inchbald. Godwin instantly reassures her. He had been "enamored of Alderson," he writes, but is no more.

Despite Godwin's fears, love was too strong for him. He and Mary became lovers in August of that year. Despite Mary's pose as a liberated woman, she went into a fog of guilt and despair. Had she been too "easy"? Had she once again given her love to a man who would not respect her? "I am afraid to trace emotions to their source, which border on agony," she wrote to Godwin the next day. She was afraid, she wrote, "that full of your own feelings . . . you forgot mine, or do not understand my character."

But Godwin's answer the next day was filled with love and gratitude. To the woman who had ended his secret terror that he was inadequate as a man, he wrote:

You do not know how honest I am. I . . . told you . . . the truth when I described to you the manner in which you set my imagination on fire on Saturday. For six and thirty hours I could think of nothing else. I longed inexpressibly to hold you in my arms. . . .

The course of love flowed tumultuously. Mary alternated between love and terror, hope and remorse. She had been too long independent, too badly hurt to commit her heart. "At 15 I resolved never to marry from interested motives," she wrote Godwin,

> or to endure a life of dependence. . . . My entire confidence in Mr. Imlay plunged me into some difficulties. . . . I know that many of my cares would have been the natural consequence of what nine out of ten would have termed folly—yet I cannot coincide in the opinion, without feeling contempt for mankind. In short, I must reckon on doing some good, and getting the money I want by my writings, or go to sleep forever.

It was October before she signed a note to Godwin with the word "love"—and then she coyly crossed it out so that it was barely visible. But as she pulled back, Godwin became more determined and finally, on December 23, she wrote happily: "Was not yesterday a very pleasant evening? There was a tenderness in your manner, as you seemed to be opening your heart, that rendered you very dear to me."

Just before the New Year, Mary discovered she was pregnant. She had wished more than anything to have Godwin's child, but the thought of telling him terrified her. Suppose he were to behave as Imlay had? She couldn't bear that heartbreak a second time! In a burst of anger, fear, she poured out the news to Godwin, blaming both of them, offering Godwin the chance to get out of the relationship and leaving her to assume all the responsibility. But she had underestimated Godwin, his character, and his love for her.

"You treated me last night with extreme unkindness," he wrote the day after she had confided her pregnancy. "You wished we had never met, you wished you could cancel all that has passed between us. Is this—ask your own heart—is this compatible with the passion of love?"

Both Mary and Godwin had strong objections to marriage and had made their views widely known. Mary had already borne one child out of wedlock. (Even if she had wanted to marry Imlay, she could not have; France had already passed the Law of Suspects decree in September 1793, making the marriage of an Englishwoman in France impossible.) But with another baby on the way, Mary began to think her position over. Could she flout society for the second time, bring up an illegitimate baby in heavily moral England, subject it to all the scorn that would fall on its innocent little head? Mary and Godwin made a thoughtful decision. Despite their theories opposing marriage, marry they must—and in allowing each other complete independence they would set an example for the rest of the world of what an ideal marriage could be.

The marriage took place on March 29, in church. Immediately after the ceremony the bride and groom returned to live in their separate establishments. Yet in spite of all their professed independence—"I wish you, from my soul, to be rivetted in my heart, but I do not desire to have you always at my elbow"—it was a completely romantic, protective marriage. Mary was sublimely happy in her pregnancy—happier than she ever had been in her whole life. "I begin to love this little creature," she wrote about the baby in the seventh month of her pregnancy, "and to anticipate his birth as a fresh twist to a knot which I do not wish to untie. . . . I love you better than I supposed I did when I promised to love you forever."

Godwin, so long the bachelor, took to approaching fatherhood with all his heart. Tenderly he worried about Mary; tactfully, so as not to crowd her, he protected her. "I think it not right, Mama, that you should walk alone in the middle of the day. Will you indulge me in the pleasure of walking with you?" he wrote in the last month of her pregnancy.

Mary did not anticipate any trouble when the time came for her to deliver the baby. After all, it was her second, and Fanny's had been such an easy, natural birth. Godwin, about to become a father for the first time at forty, was more apprehensive. He suggested that Mary be attended by a doctor rather than the midwife, Mrs. Belkinsop, that Mary had chosen. Mary was insistent. She was too much a feminist to think a man trained as a physician would be better than a woman midwife who had her natural instincts to help her. Determined, Mary won out over her husband's objections, and when she began to go into labor on August 29, Godwin was sent to fetch Mrs. Belkinsop.

It was the most tragic mistake of her life—and, in fact, it probably cost her her life. The delivery began slowly, and although the midwife reassured her everything would be all right, Mary worried. In her last note, on August 30, 1797, she wrote—poignantly echoing the expression that had been her own mother's last words: "Mrs. Belkinsop tells me that I am in the most natural state, and can promise me a safe delivery—but *I must have a little patience.*"

The new Mary was born late the following night. The rest of the story is Godwin's—he told it heartbreakingly in his diary, and again in his *Memoirs.* Mary Wollstonecraft lingered for twelve hideous days, feverish, agonized with pain, falling in and out of delirium. Godwin's friends sat disheveled about the house, eager to go on helpful errands while the terrible slow process dragged on. At last, early on the morning of September 10, mercifully, Mary was released. Godwin, unable to write the fact of her death in his diary, simply entered the words "20 minutes before 8" and filled in three lines with strokes of his pen.

She was buried in the churchyard of St. Pancras where five months earlier she had been married. Godwin saw to the preparation of a gray stone memorial inscribed:

Mary Wollstonecraft Godwin
Author of
A Vindication of the Rights of Woman
Born 27th April 1759
Died 10th September 1797

Then, at last, he went back home to begin the task that Mary Wollstonecraft so tragically had not been able to complete—the rearing of the tiny girl who bore her mother's name.

3

The Portrait
over the Mantel

Sometimes Mary thought that the portrait over the mantel was her only friend.

She would sit quietly in the parlor of the house on Skinner Street, shutting out the voices of the other children and her stepmother, and talk in whispers to the beautiful face in the oval frame.

If only her mother were alive! The portrait told her everything; Mary Wollstonecraft Godwin's painted eyes, loving and wise, smiled down on her little girl. In that face was all that Mary yearned for—compassion, tenderness, a lovely, strong-chinned, high-cheekboned visage, courageous, alive, surrounded by an aureole of flame-red hair, legacies of the fire and wit of the older Mary's Irish ancestors.

It was so lonely without her! William Godwin had known when his wife died that he was not cut out to raise an orphaned stepdaughter and a tiny new baby of his own. He cursed the fate that left him "the most unfit person for this office"—that of raising Mary in place of her mother who was "the best qualified in the world."

Godwin had tried parenthood once—in a way. When he was still a young man and struggling to make a career for himself as a writer, he became foster father to a twelve-year-old, Thomas Cooper, a distant relative. Thomas was educated by Godwin according to the progressive ideas developed by Jean Jacques Rousseau in his book, *Emile*: Education should follow the natural curiosity of the student; all teaching should be based on sincerity and plain speaking between student and teacher, rather than on formal study and rigid discipline. But although Tom and Godwin were together until the boy left to become a strolling player at seventeen, and later letters testified to a real warmth and friendship between them, Godwin felt he had failed with Tom. His philosophic calm had broken down when he was tested with the boy's mischief and high spirits, and despite his resolve never to punish his ward, often his voice would rise and sometimes his fists would fly.

Mary Wollstonecraft, on the other hand, was a natural mother. Before they were married Godwin often would sit in Mary's parlor and watch her play with her first daughter, Fanny, cuddle her, tell her stories, listen with intense seriousness to the baby's first words. What a parent Mary would have made for this new little Mary—and how unfair it seemed to Godwin that she had died and left the job to him!

Godwin had spent his first forty years as a bachelor.

But when he fell in love with Mary Wollstonecraft, he knew he could never live without a woman again. In a panic of loneliness and grief, he began at once to seek a wife. He wooed, as ardently as his cool nature allowed, first Mrs. Ravenel, a neighbor, and then Maria Reveley, Mary Wollstonecraft's friend. Both women promptly rejected him. Finally, his last opportunity appeared in the plump and rather coarse-featured form of his next-door neighbor, Mary Jane Clairmont. "Is it possible I behold the immortal Godwin?" Mrs. Clairmont asked archly; and, flattered and relieved, Godwin shortly took her to be his wife.

Mrs. Clairmont was a long step down from Mary Wollstonecraft. Mary later described her as "illiterate, vulgar, coarse-minded though good-natured." Besides, once the thrill of having captured "the immortal" William Godwin wore out, Mrs. Clairmont discovered that she had a heavy cargo to carry. She already had two small children—Charles and Jane, who was just Mary's age—and now there were five-year-old Fanny and two-year-old little Mary. Shortly there would be William, her child with Godwin. The house was small and cluttered with Godwin's papers and books; there was scarcely any money, so that the whole burden of keeping house and caring for the children fell solely on her. And finally, there was Godwin himself—beloved and respected by a wide circle of friends, people with whom the new Mrs. Godwin had nothing at all in common, but rather remote and lofty and not inclined to sit down over a cup of tea and easy gossip with his wife.

Godwin's friends saw his second wife in different colors: Charles Lamb, the essayist and coauthor of

Lamb's *Tales from Shakespeare*, privately called her a "damn'd infernal bitch," while Aaron Burr described her as an "amiable" woman. But however she struck the world at large, Mrs. Godwin was lonely, overworked, worried about making ends meet in a household with five children—and inclined to take out her troubles on Mary.

Mary was fair game. Fanny was a docile child, anxious to please, a sad-eyed, gentle little thing who carried her loneliness around silently with her and caused harried Mrs. Godwin virtually no trouble. Mary was another matter: argumentative, critical, moody. She was, in fact, a lot like her mother. At least she had her mother's faults: She was a worrier. Her father, describing her character later, complained that she had "the practice of seeing everything on the gloomy side," and once in fact put it squarely to her: "I am afraid you are a Wollstonecraft." Even if Mrs. Godwin had tried, she would have found it hard to win Mary's heart.

But she never tried at all. Clearly her own daughter, Jane—who later changed her name to Claire—was her favorite. Mary was cool, pale, reserved. Claire was dramatic, vivid, a beautiful child with a lilting singing voice. While Mary would go off by herself, Claire was at center stage. High-spirited, witty, a perfect mimic, Claire would convulse the grown-ups—and the house was always full of them, comrades and disciples of Godwin's—with her dramatics. She was also hot-tempered and hysterical and given to imaginary crises which would put the household on edge, but her mother, clearly enchanted by her vivid offspring, coddled Claire as much as her limited time allowed. While she resented Mary's small fits of petulance, she made endless excuses for Claire. When the two little girls fought—and fight they did, constantly—it was always Claire who was right and Mary who was wrong.

Mary would awaken in the morning to the slam-bang sounds of a household in riotous activity—bustling, bossy Mrs. Godwin barking out orders, Claire up to her tricks and preparing to have a tantrum if they didn't work, Fanny timidly trying to make peace, while Godwin escaped it all closed in his study. The conflict would begin at once. Her stepmother had a full program for Mary—set the table for breakfast, help with the washing up, a dozen other chores fastidious Mary detested. What she really wanted to do had to be sandwiched in somehow—read, dream, write some poems and stories, live in a world of her own creation that only her mother would have understood.

While Mary's stepmother managed the household with her heavy hand, Godwin took over the education of the three girls (the boys were sent to school). He was following Mary Wollstonecraft's ideas as she had explained them in *Thoughts on the Education of Daughters*: "If a mother has leisure and good sense, and more than one daughter, I think she could best educate them herself." In line with Mary Wollstonecraft's theories that education should be planned but not rigid—"The mind is not, cannot be created by the teacher, though it may be cultivated and its real powers found out"— Godwin educated each of his daughters differently. Although he was scrupulously fair in his behavior— he treated Fanny Imlay exactly as though she were his own daughter, and in fact hid from her the knowledge that she wasn't—his analytic eye saw Mary as the most promising of his children. She was given the greatest scope in her studies: the classics, astronomy, mathematics, logic, the new humanistic philosophy based on the work of Rousseau, Voltaire, and Godwin himself. With a father who was one of the intellectual giants of his day, Mary had every advantage in expanding her own worthy intelligence.

Yet despite all the blessings of her heredity and the environment that Godwin created, things at home did not go well for Mary—nor for that matter for the family in general. Sensitive Mary knew somehow that her father never really got over the loss of the woman who had brought tenderness and passion into his life. A strange and terrible change of fate swept over him when Mary Wollstonecraft died. Not only was love lost, but oddly, at exactly the same time, his luster as a thinker and writer began to dim. Mary herself wrote about it later:

> All outward things seemed to have lost their existence . . . to him. . . . This towering spirit who had excited interest and high expectation in all who knew and could value him, became at once, as it were extinct. He existed from this moment for himself only. His friends remembered him as a brilliant vision which would never again return to them.

Godwin continued to write—in fact, his first work after Mary Wollstonecraft's death was a four-volume biography, *Memoirs of the Author of a Vindication of the Rights of Woman*—but none of his other works had the same impact as the books he wrote before her death.

Then, too, money, always a problem for writers and

intellectuals, whose work may be widely appreciated but is usually hopelessly underpaid, never went far enough in a household with two adults and five hungry children—not to mention scores of friends who always somehow stayed to dinner. Mrs. Godwin nagged, complained, and finally decided the only thing to do was to take matters into her own hands. She persuaded Godwin to become a publisher of children's books. Together they opened an establishment on Skinner Street in Holborn, and set to work as a business partnership.

The publishing venture that was to save them from the poorhouse soon became another mouth to feed. Printers needed to be paid, writers' royalties had to be distributed. Bossy Mrs. Godwin thought she was a born businesswoman; it soon was clear that she was not. Worse, she decided that she knew more about literature than Godwin did, and as a result the only book of note that issued from Skinner Street was *Tales from Shakespeare* by the Lambs.

While the publishing house was bolstered by loans from friends, the household, too, was lifted by inspired company. Godwin's disciples continued to come to his home. Among them were the most imaginative and creative people in England. One night a note arrived from Samuel Taylor Coleridge, the poet. He had revised his poem *The Rime of the Ancient Mariner*. Could he come over, he asked, and read it to Godwin?

Mary was thrilled. Coleridge was handsome, magnetic; he had a magical voice. She ran off to find Fanny. The two girls made a plan. They would hide behind the sofa where Mrs. Godwin would be unlikely to discover them, and eavesdrop on the reading.

The careful maneuver was quickly defeated. Sharp-eyed Mrs. Godwin spotted something amiss. She pulled the sofa from the wall triumphantly, exposing the two shamefaced little girls crouched behind it. "Come out at once," she directed, and only Coleridge's pleading for the children allowed them to stay for the treat. Even Mrs. Godwin could not resist the hypnotic persuasion of that wonderful voice!

Charles Lamb, the writer and critic, was also a friend to Mary and the other children. He delighted in amusing them. One night at dinner he suddenly leaned over and blew out the candle. In the dark, he picked up the cold leg of mutton from the table and put it in the hand of one of the guests. When the candle was relit, Lamb shook his head chidingly. "Martin, Martin," he said in a voice heavy with disappointment, "I never should have thought it of you."

Mary thought Lamb's next prank was even funnier. One day, while nobody was looking, he stole a cruet from the table. Mrs. Godwin missed it just after he left and questioned each of the children. When it was clear nobody had seen it, she began to search through cupboards and sideboards—but the cruet seemed magically to have disappeared. The next day Lamb walked in quietly as usual, and while the family was deep in conversation, he pulled the cruet from his pocket, put it on the table, and continued talking as though nothing had happened!

But these light moments in the company of her father's entrancing friends—and the magic times he took her to lectures, the theater, and concerts—were only occasional breaks in Mary's lonely childhood. It was not that her father didn't try to understand her, for indeed he did. It was simply that except for a brief time in his life when he was married to Mary Wollstonecraft, he found it hard to get into a close relationship with another human being. Clearly, he loved Mary—probably more than he had loved anyone except her mother—but he couldn't show it. He couldn't put his arms around her, snuggle her, comfort her when she cried as her mother would have, partly because it was not in his nature, and partly because there were already too many emotional currents—jealousy, competitiveness, scenes, and hysterics—at work in that household. Mrs. Godwin viewed Mary as a potential rival for her husband's interest and affections, and Godwin wanted to keep peace at any price.

By the time Mary was fourteen, it all began to tell on her. One day she woke up with odd sensations in her arm. The ailment was diagnosed as "nerve trouble." Her father decided that the best cure was to send Mary away from London, into the fresh country air of Ramsgate. Mary's six months away from home restored her spirits and her health. She returned to Skinner Street in time for Christmas, pink, healthy, happy—and glad to see her family again.

It was not to last long. Within a month or two all the old tensions came back. But this time luck was with Mary. Charles Clairmont, her stepbrother, had gone to work in Edinburgh, Scotland, and there he met a family named Baxter. Mr. Baxter was a hardheaded, methodical businessman with a large heart and an interest in philosophy. He had long admired Godwin's work and had known Godwin slightly for about five years. On a visit to the Godwin house, Baxter's canny eye saw it all too clearly. Mary, he thought, was beginning to wilt in the stuffy air of Skinner Street, and the kindly man invited her to come and stay with his wife and daughters for an indefinite period.

The invitation to Scotland was just what Mary needed. In a fever of excitement, she packed her dresses, books, diaries—and took temporary leave of the portrait over the mantel. Even the sea voyage to Dundee didn't dim her fever—although she was wretchedly seasick and worried whether she would even live to see Scotland's shores!

Back at home, Mary's absence was both a relief and worry to her father. In the privacy of his study he poured out his feelings of love for Mary, and his guilt, because he knew that Mary's melancholy was at least partly his fault, in a touching letter to Mr. Baxter:

"The old proverb says, 'He is a wise father who knows his own child' and I feel the justice of the apothegm on the present occasion," Godwin wrote. Apologetically, he continued: "There never can be a perfect equality between father and child," particularly "if he has other objects and avocations to fill up the greater part of his time." A father, then, Godwin continued, was likely "to proclaim his wishes and commands in a[n] . . . authoritative [way] and . . . can . . . seldom [be] . . . the confidant of his child." Looking at their relationship from Mary's point of view, he continued, it was natural that the child would "feel some degree of awe or restraint. . . . I am not, therefore, a perfect judge of Mary's character. I believe that she has nothing of what is commonly called vices, and that she has considerable talent."

In his letters Godwin felt free to show what he was so careful to hide at home: Mary was his favorite.

My own daughter is considerably superior in capacity to the one her mother had before. Fanny, the eldest, is of a quiet, modest, unshowy disposition. . . . Mary, my daughter, is the reverse of her in many particulars. She is singularly bold, somewhat imperious, and active of mind. Her desire of knowledge is great, and her perseverance in everything she undertakes almost invincible. My own daughter is, I believe, very pretty."

Mary knew nothing of her father's confession, but she did know that for the first time in her life, she wasn't at all lonely. She felt surrounded by love, which her own family withheld from her. The Baxters were warm and easygoing. Isabel, the daughter closest to her own age, and Mary immediately became intimate friends. Even the older sister, Christy, didn't talk down to her, or treat her as though she were in the way.

And life in Dundee was so pleasant! Open countryside replaced the dingy streets of London. There was swimming, hiking, picnic lunches—trees to climb, brooks to wade in, grassy hills that she could roll down. The closest connection Mary had at home with the country was the cemetery in which her mother was buried—and she had in recent years taken to stealing off there to sit at her mother's grave among the trees and in the quiet of the graveyard. But here she could be close to the beauty of nature and surrounded not by death, but by life—lively companions, gaiety, pure fun.

As the weeks went by—she stayed for five months with the Baxters—Mary felt she had become a part of their family. She missed gentle Fanny, and her talks with her father, but it was such a relief to be away from bossy Mrs. Godwin and demanding Claire. When the time came to go back, Mary suddenly felt frightened. The sensitive Baxters immediately came up with a solution: Mary's transition back to Skinner Street would be softened if she took Christy along with her for a return visit.

If Mary had worried about the effect her return would have on the family, she need not have. Here she had been gone for five months, and now her welcome home was under the shadow of what Godwin considered a far more important event: The household was in a frenzy of preparation for a visit from a twenty-year-old poet named Percy Bysshe Shelley!

Mary and Christy took a cool view of the furor. Shelley's expected visit the next day might excite Godwin, but it made no impression on them! Mary was even a little snide; her father, she knew, genius or not, was human enough to be flattered by a letter from a rich young poet, the rebellious son of a rich and titled family, that began:

The name of Godwin has been used to excite in me feelings of reverence and admiration, I have been accustomed to consider him a luminary too dazzling for the darkness which surrounds him; From the earliest period of my knowledge of his principles I have ardently desired to share on the footing of intimacy that intellect which I have delighted to contemplate in its emanations. Con-

sidering then these feelings you will not be surprised at the inconceivable emotions with which
I learned your existence and your dwelling. I had
enrolled your name in the list of the honourable
dead. I had felt regret that the glory of your being
had passed from this earth of ours. It is not so.
You still live, and I firmly believe you are still
planning the welfare of human kind.

Worse than her father's succumbing to flattery,
Mary thought, was a quality in Godwin that secretly
shamed her: Godwin's willingness to borrow
money—that he had no intention of repaying—from
his richer friends and admirers. For Godwin there
was no inconsistency in his noble ideals about humanity and his beggarly tapping of other people's funds:
Was he not a social theorist who genuinely believed
that wealth should be distributed among all the people
to benefit mankind, not held in the hands of a few to
be spent on greedy pleasures? Mary, though, like her
mother before her, saw Godwin's money scrounging
as a flaw in an otherwise noble character. Shelley, she
had heard, was rich; she knew that her father was
planning to hit him up for money to rescue his publishing house and provide for his family, and Mary
didn't want to be around when it all took place! She
and Christy would make themselves as scarce as possible, so as to avoid any confrontation with Shelley.

The girls' plan was almost successful. Mary and
Shelley caught only a fleeting glimpse of each other.
Nor was either impressed. Mary saw a tall, stooped
young man with a halo of golden hair around an oddly
sensual face, while Shelley saw a pale, fair-haired little

girl with big, solemn gray eyes. Only Shelley's young wife, Harriet, was impressive. Christy wrote in her diary that she was exquisitely beautiful—with her "brilliant complexion set off to perfection by her vivid purple satin dress." Shelley, Harriet, and the two girls were introduced and spoke only for a moment or two; then, as quickly as manners permitted, Mary and Christy excused themselves.

Christy's visit was over all too quickly, and Mary took up her lonely life on Skinner Street again. More and more she turned to Fanny for understanding and friendship. Fanny, a petite, white-skinned young woman with golden curls and clear, honest blue eyes, didn't look much like Mary Wollstonecraft, and she lacked the high spirit and intense courage that her mother had possessed, but like the first Mary, she was loyal to those she loved, and generous with her feelings. Then, too, she had more than Mary to remember her mother by—Mary had only the portrait, a locket, and few trinkets that her father had told her belonged to Mary Wollstonecraft. Fanny, who was three when their mother died, had memories of a beautiful red-haired woman who would sleep sometimes with Fanny cuddled in her arms, play with her, tell her stories. Mary and Fanny would sit together for hours and go over the dimly recalled memories of the mother they both missed so much.

Mary's dark moods deepened once again in the tense atmosphere of the house on Skinner Street. This time Godwin knew how to cope; he made arrangements for Mary to return to Dundee, where he knew the wholesome Baxters would bring Mary back to herself. Mary's visit was to be longer this time—she stayed in Scotland on and off for two years.

It was a pale, solemn little girl who went off to Scotland, awkward and carelessly dressed. The person who returned in 1814 was a young woman of sixteen, with nothing of the gawky adolescent about her. Mary had matured, her thin little body had filled out, become slender and graceful. The portraits of her a few years later show her as Sophia Stately described her, a "sweet pretty woman," with what the poet Leigh Hunt called a "great tablet of a forehead," and fair hair "of a sunny and burnished brightness" falling "like a golden network around her face and throat." Even more striking was the impression she left: According to Robert Owen, a friend of the family who would become one of the fathers of socialism, her face, "though not regularly beautiful, was comely and spiritual, of winning expression, and with a look of inborn refinement as well as culture."

Shelley thought her beautiful from the very start. "White, bright and clear," she was then, as Christy Baxter remembered her. In the two years she had been away, Shelley had become a regular visitor at Skinner Street. His marriage had fallen upon hard times. His romantic love for his wife, Harriet, had given way to an endless round of bickering over Harriet's extravagance, her frivolous tastes, her dependence on her sister, Eliza, whom Shelley hated. Shelley had left her several times; he had even had a brief romance with a woman named Cornelia Boinville. Finding his own home, as he wrote in his poem "Away," "sad and silent," he increasingly sought refuge in Godwin's. Mary knew about this—Fanny had written to her while she was in Scotland—and she was prepared to find Shelley there. What she was not prepared for, though, was the swift and certain way in which she and Shelley would fall in love!

Shelley was forewarned. As early as 1812, Godwin had written to Shelley saying: "You cannot imagine how much all the females of my family—Mrs. Godwin and three daughters—are interested in your history." If that was not enough to kindle Shelley's volatile, romantic heart, the fact that Mary was the child of the woman his idealistic imagination had set up as a deity surely was. "What is it he sees in her?" a friend later asked—and the answer was "[H]er name was Mary, and not only Mary, but Mary Wollstonecraft."

No wonder, then, the second sight of Mary made Shelley feel a dream had come true—"a dream from heaven."

Mary was different from any girl Shelley had ever met. Her fairness and poise were in contrast to Claire's dark, exotic wildness, to the gentle shyness of Fanny, and to the rosy bloom of pink-and-white Harriet. In Shelley's stormy emotional life, Mary was an oasis of calm. "Gentle and good and mild thou art," he told her in a poem he wrote to her the summer that they fell in love. "So soothing, so powerful and quiet are your expressions that it is almost like folding you to my heart," he wrote to her later.

While Shelley saw a cool, tranquil goddess, Mary saw the poet as a tragic and betrayed man. His brilliance as a poet was under a cloud because of his unhappy marriage, she thought. Shelley had married Harriet with the idea of molding her into his ideal woman, he told Mary. Now, his wife had betrayed him. Not only had she refused to be the woman of intellect and ideals that he could love, Shelley had reason to believe that she had been unfaithful to him. He was sure that Harriet had given herself to another man—a soldier named Major Ryan.

Shelley knew that Mary used to take her favorite books and escape to her mother's grave in the St. Pancras churchyard, where she could spend her most sacred moments of solitude. He followed her there one day. Sitting as close to Mary as he dared, he poured his heart out to her. He told her about his own childhood—in a way as difficult as her own, for despite his high-born position, Shelley was a rebel who always felt "on the outside" in society. He, too, was lonely, filled with romantic visions, seeking a world of ideas and harmony.

Mary was frightened, exalted, fascinated. Shelley, who had seemed so odd-looking the first time she had seen him, now appeared to her romantically handsome. Each day brought a meeting with him. He would appear at the grave, throw himself on the grass with his head in Mary's lap, and recite his wonderful poetry to her. He brought a copy of *Queen Mab*, a long philosophic poem he had written, and wrote in the flyleaf: "You see Mary, I have not forgotten you." Mary took it home, hid it, and then added on the last page of the volume:

July 1814. This book is sacred to me, and as no other creature shall ever look into it, I may write in it what I please—yet what shall I write?—that I love the author beyond all the powers of expression, and that I am parted from him, dearest and only love—by that love we have promised to each other, although I may not be yours, I can never be another's. But I am thine, exclusively thine.

By the kiss of love, the glance none saw beside,
The smile none else might understand,
The whispered thought of hearts allied,
The pressure of the thrilling hand.

I have pledged myself to thee, and sacred is the gift. I remember your words: "You are now, Mary, going to mix with many, and for a moment I shall depart, but in the solitude of your chamber, I shall be with you." Yes, you are ever with me, sacred vision.

But ah! I feel in this was given
A blessing never meant for me,
Thou art too like a dream from heaven
For earthly love to merit thee!

Shelley could not confide his love of Mary to anyone—he was still bound to Harriet. But he could not keep it to himself, either. He needed to give a clue, a hint of what he felt. He made arrangements to meet his friend Thomas Jefferson Hogg at nearby Cheapside, and they walked together to Godwin's home and shop on Skinner Street.

Just as Shelley had hoped, Godwin was not at home. He and Hogg waited for a few minutes and then, according to Hogg,

The door was partially and softly opened. A thrilling voice called "Shelley." A thrilling voice answered, "Mary!" And he darted out of the room like an arrow from the bow of the far-shooting king. A very young female, fair and fair-haired, wearing a frock of tartan, an unusual dress in London at that time, had called him out of the room. He was absent a very short time—a minute or two, and then returned.

Shelley's purpose was accomplished. "Godwin is out, there is no use in waiting," he told his friend.

As Shelley knew he would, Hogg asked the question: "Who was that, pray?"

"A daughter."

"A daughter of William Godwin?"

"The daughter of Godwin and Mary," Shelley replied.

But while Shelley was occupied with deliciously dangerous games, Harriet had no such diversions. She had gone out of town, but by July 14 she returned to confront her husband. Why, she wanted to know, had he not written to her?

Shelley, caught in the torment of his now total love for Mary and his guilt about the wife he no longer cared for, sent out an urgent call to his friend, Thomas Peacock. "Come at once," he wrote.

It was a distraught Shelley who opened the door to admit his friend. His eyes were bloodshot, his clothes disordered. "Nothing that I ever read in tales or history could . . . present a more striking image of a sudden, violent, uncontrollable passion than that under which I found him labouring," Peacock described the scene later.

Between his old feeling for Harriet, *from whom he was not then separated*, and his new passion for Mary, he showed in his looks, in his gestures, in his speech, the state of a mind suffering "like a little kingdom, the nature of an insurrection."

Shelley began to speak, almost incoherently, about his love for Mary. Then, suddenly, he reached into his pocket and took out a bottle of laudanum—an opiate that in overdose was poison. "I never part from this," he shouted, waving the bottle about. He began to pace around the room. "I am always repeating your lines from Sophocles:

> Man's happiest lot is not to be;
> And when we tread life's thorny steep
> Most blessed are they, who earliest free
> Descend to earth's eternal sleep."

Behind all his histrionics, Shelley was genuinely baffled and rather annoyed. He had no anger toward Harriet, no wish to hurt her, no thought of divorce or even permanent separation. His passion for her was over, but he was willing to accept her in another way—as a sister. Her wish to keep the marriage intact he interpreted as mere jealousy and possessiveness, and he thought that sooner or later she would get over it. Shelley was simply unable to conceive of the fact that other people did not always feel exactly as he did!

This quality—ascribing to others the emotions he himself felt—also motivated his behavior toward Godwin. Shelley decided to return to Mary and confront her father with the fact of their love toward each other. Some arrangement would be worked out, he

54

told Mary. Godwin would understand—had he not written about "free love," describing marriage as a bondage, insisting that the only sacred ties between man and woman were the ties of love? Together he and Mary made plans to tell her father and to ask for his blessings.

Godwin's reaction was unexpected, violent, and bitter. Mary was not yet seventeen, while Shelley was twenty-two, a married man, and a father himself. Furiously, Mary's father accused him of seducing his daughter, carrying out a love affair behind his back! What would be Mary's fate with this erratic, dishonorable man? Godwin stormed. What he wanted for Mary was what every father, philosopher or not, wanted: happiness, security, the respect of friends and community.

Mary was less surprised than Shelley at Godwin's reaction, but she was deeply troubled. It was impossible now to continue to meet at her mother's grave; the romance that was so sweet because it was a secret now could become a matter of lies and concealment. But to end it was unthinkable! She and Shelley were madly in love—there was no life for either of them apart.

There was only one way—and whatever the price was, Mary was willing to pay it. She began to make hasty plans with Shelley. Together they paid a last visit to her mother's grave—the mother that Mary knew somehow would have understood, would have been on her side. Then, quietly but resolutely, Mary went back to the house on Skinner Street to pack her diaries and a few clothes, and to whisper good-bye to the house she was probably leaving forever.

4

The Runaways

The sun had barely risen on the dawn of a brooding summer day, July 28, 1814, when two girls slipped quietly out of the house on Skinner Street. On the corner a carriage was waiting. Breathlessly, Mary and Claire climbed in. Shelley called out an order to the driver and within a few minutes the trio was safe—on the road to Dover!

Mary and Shelley had confided in Claire about their elopement. Then, at the last moment, an impulsive decision was made. Claire was fluent in French. She would be the translator for the couple on the continent. In a fever of excitement, the lovers agreed to take her along.

The journey was terrifying for Mary. Shelley records it in all its misery and wild anticipation in the joint diary he and Mary began on that day:

Mary was ill as we travelled, yet in that illness what pleasure and security did we not share! The heat made her faint; it was necessary at every stage that she should repose. I was divided between anxiety for her health and terror lest our pursuers should arrive.

At Dartford we took four horses, that we might outstrip pursuit. We arrived at Dover before 4 o'clock . . . we engaged a small boat to convey us to Calais. . . . The evening was most beautiful; the sands slowly receded; we felt safe; there was little wind. . . . The moon rose, the night came on, and with the night a slow heavy swell and a fresher breeze, which soon became so violent as to toss the boat very much. Mary was much affected by the sea, she could scarcely move. She lay in my arms through the night; the little strength which remained to my own exhausted frame was all expended in keeping her head in rest on my bosom. The wind was violent and contrary . . . a thunder squall struck the sail and the waves rushed into the boat. . . .

Mary did not know our danger; she was resting between my knees, that were unable to support her; she did not speak or look, but I felt that she was there. . . .

The morning broke, the lightning died away, the violence of the wind abated. We arrived at Calais, whilst Mary still slept; we drove upon the sands. Suddenly the broad sun rose over France.

Mary, Shelley, and Claire were jubilant. They had made the break—Mary to take the major step of her life, from adolescence in a stifling home to independent adulthood with the man she loved; Shelley to live out his dream of life with a companion who "can feel poetry and understand philosophy"; and Claire to seek the adventure her mischievous spirit needed. Even Mrs. Godwin's arrival by packet boat the next day—they heard from the hotel porter that a "fat lady" was looking for the man who "had run away with her daughter"—did not deter the trio. Claire spent the night with her mother and sent her back alone to London.

Free at last, Mary's rapturous heart sang! Nothing could harm her, she knew. Shelley, too, was buoyed by her trust: "She feels as if our love would alone suffice to resist the invasions of calamity," he wrote in their journal.

"Invasions of calamity" was accurate, indeed! It took only three days for Mary to discover that Shelley, with his romantic disregard of practical matters, had left London with no money. An English "milord" in Paris had certain advantages, however, Mary discovered. Shelley sold his watch and chain, borrowed some money from a French businessman, sent Mary and Claire to the livestock market to buy a donkey to carry their traveling bag. Thus equipped, the three set out to walk to Switzerland.

More trouble followed. The donkey, who was intended to carry Mary and her bag, broke down; they had to sell him and buy a mule. Mary was not to ride the mule, either; a few days later Shelley sprained his foot. He became the passenger while Mary and Claire in their black silk dresses—the only ones they had taken with them—trudged alongside over the rutted French roads.

Night was scarcely better. Shelley wrote, "we slept at a little old woman's whose beds were infinitely detestable," but fastidious Mary was more to the point. "Let me observe that we here discovered that the inhabitants were not in the habit of washing themselves either when they rose or went to bed," and then, the next day, Claire "was not able to sleep all night for the rats who as she said put their cold paws on her face." At Echemine, "the cabaret we rested at was not equalled by any description I have heard of an Irish cabin in filth, and certainly the dirtiest Scotch cottage I ever entered was exquisitely clean beside it." At Troyes the travelers got "into a dirty apartment of a nasty auberge to sleep," and it was not until they reached Pontarlier, ten days later, that Mary wrote, "We sleep, for the first time in France, in a clean bed."

Yet, despite the heat, dust, and dirt, Mary was happier than she had ever been. She fell into Shelley's mood—living entirely for the moment. They stopped as the wish hit them, to picnic beside some beautiful scene, to read aloud from the one or two books they had taken with them, to write in the journal. Mary had brought along a box of papers—her own writings, letters from her father and her friends, and Shelley's love letters written while they were apart during the spring of their courtship. The box was lost in Paris and never recovered—much to Mary's and Shelley's sorrow—but Mary had another idea. Shelley was encouraging her to work on a novel, oddly entitled *Hate*, and she was anxious to talk over her ideas with him, work under his tutelage and encouragement. Shelley, too, was at work. He began a prose romance called *The*

Assassins—a happier and more optimistic story than the title suggests. Taking down his words on a chilly, rainy day at Brunnen, Mary knew that they were a description of the ecstasy she brought into his life: "The very winds breathed health and renovation . . . and the joyousness of youthful courage."

The adventure of the honeymoon and the delight of their love—"Mary slept in my arms," Shelley wrote again and again in the journal—helped the lovers to forget temporarily the tangled web of legal, financial, and family troubles they had left behind in England.

Most pressing was the problem of Harriet. Shelley was racked with guilt, now even more troubling because Harriet was pregnant. At one point during the journey he even wrote to her, "I urge you to come to Switzerland, where you will at least find one firm & constant friend, to whom your interests will always be dear, by whom your feelings will never be wilfully injured." Harriet, quite naturally, chose not to come. Instead she continued to run up bills at shops and have the accounts held for Shelley.

Money was the second problem. Shelley had borrowed against his future inheritance—post-obits, as the notes were called—chiefly to fund Godwin, but also for his own needs. The rates of interest were ruinous and Shelley was to spend much of his life hiding from bailiffs who were out to arrest him for default of debts.

Then, too, there was Godwin's unwillingness to forget the hurt that Mary and Shelley had dealt to his vanity both as a father and a philosopher. Mary suffered heavily because she felt she had abandoned him, and also because she knew her father thought he had been made a fool of. Here he was, world famous as a moralist, and now he was seen as a man who could not order his own household! On the one hand Mary felt guilty, and on the other disappointed in her father's behavior.

And last—and possibly most painful to Mary—was her feeling of having betrayed Fanny. Mary had been afraid to confide in her, knowing that Fanny, in her need to protect her younger sister, might have tried to persuade Mary not to run away. It was simpler at the time to take Claire into her confidence and leave Fanny out. Now, away from home, Mary was torn with the knowledge that Fanny must be deeply wounded by Mary's secrecy.

Even hundreds of miles away from home, separated from England by the mountains and the sea, Mary found her life still linked to home. Shelley had outlined a list of books to read and study with her. Highest on this list were Mary Wollstonecraft's and Godwin's works, which he and Mary had each read before, and were to read again and again all their lives. Mary Wollstonecraft's *Letters Written During a Short Residence in Denmark, Norway, and Sweden*, completed the year her daughter was born, and an autobiographical novel published posthumously, *Mary, a Fiction*, were favorite reading. The couple went through both volumes of Godwin's *Political Justice* and all three volumes of his novel *Caleb Williams.*

Reading aloud with Shelley was one way to be alone with him, Mary discovered. What a joy to have Claire out of the way! Mary walked a careful line; Claire sometimes exasperated Shelley, she knew, but she amused him too. Besides, Claire and Shelley shared something that Mary had in short supply—physical energy. Sometimes Mary, exhausted by the frenetic pace, felt her strength running out and needed to retreat to a quiet place to rest and read. Claire and Shelley, like mischievous children, would run off together on an excursion while Mary, torn by jealousy, held her tongue. Claire's intrusion went even further than these jaunts. Often at night she would become "frightened"; rats were running over her bed, or she was pursued by ghosts and visions, she would explain in the middle of the night. Nothing would calm her except crawling into Mary and Shelley's "connubial bed." If only, Mary would wish, Claire would find a home with someone else!

But the decision to return—made suddenly and impulsively, as all their plans seemed to be—included Claire too. They had arrived in a village called Brunnen in Switzerland and fallen in love with its beauty. Shelley immediately took a house for six months. The contract lasted exactly twenty-four hours; sometime during the night Mary and Shelley had a serious talk about their finances, and together they came to the conclusion that the idyll was over. "Determine at last to return to England," Mary wrote in her journal. "Only wait to set off till the washerwoman brings home our linen." A short delay: "[T]he linen is not dry; we are compelled to wait until tomorrow. We engage a boat to take us to Lucerne at 6 the following morning."

To save money—and because it was the most romantic route home—the trio decided to return via the Rhine River, going back by way of Germany and Holland. On Tuesday, August 30, Mary celebrated her seventeenth birthday, "not," as she wrote, "in comfort. We expect to be, not happier, but more at our ease before the year passes." Ease, indeed, seemed a long way off. True, the trip was beautiful and exciting. "The banks of the Rhine are very fine—rocks and mountains, crowned with lonely castles. . . . A ruined tower with its desolated windows, stood on the summit of another hill that jutted into the river," Mary's diary reads. But as always, improvident Shelley had underestimated their expenses. They reached Rotterdam on September 8, "horribly cheated," with only enough money to bargain for voyage home, and arrived at Gravesend, in England, on September 13 and without a penny. They had to take the boatman into their coach and drive around London looking for money to pay him!

If Mary had hoped that her absence would make her father forget his anger, she soon found out she was wrong. Godwin, if anything, had hardened his heart even more against his favorite child. He made it perfectly clear that although he had not the slightest compunction about continuing to "borrow" money from Shelley, it would have to be at a distance. The doors of Skinner Street remained firmly closed to the lovers. Furthermore, he had laid the law down to Fanny. Under no conditions was she to see her errant sister and the man who had led her astray!

Debt, indeed, had tarnished Godwin's character. The brilliant philosopher, now nearing sixty, lived in constant fear of bankruptcy, a terror not helped by Mrs. Godwin's constant nagging. "I detest Mrs. G.," Mary wrote to Shelley in October, during one of the weeks in which he was hiding out in obscure lodgings to escape bailiffs who were out after him. "[S]he plagues my father out of his life. . . . Why will not Godwin follow the obvious bent of his affections and be reconciled to us . . . do you not hate her my love. . . ."

While Godwin remained barricaded behind his own doors, Mrs. Godwin was much in evidence. She would pay secret visits to their lodgings, peeking into their windows, "cruising up and down like an enemy squadron" and then vanishing. Mary could not imagine what reports, if any, she was carrying back to Godwin, but secretly Mary wished her success in at least one of her purposes—to reclaim Claire!

Claire was little comfort to her when things went wrong. No matter how serious Shelley's problems became—and Mary's too, because her life was linked to his—Claire continued to demand attention. No matter that Harriet was running up bills for which Shelley was responsible, that Shelley was burdened with demands from creditors and agents (his friend Peacock being one of them), that Fanny—quietly breaking the embargo laid by Godwin—had visited them to warn them about a rumor: Harriet was plotting to have Shelley arrested and Godwin ruined. Claire thought only of herself. She fastened upon Shelley by her process of being sullen and sunny in turn. Shelley would tire of her in time, Mary hoped. In the meantime, she took comfort in crumbs like this entry in Shelley's handwriting in their diary: "Oct. 14 Claire's insensibility and incapacity for the slightest degree of friendship . . . prevent me (Shelley) from maintaining any measure in severity. . . . Beware of weakly giving way to revival sympathies. Content yourself with one great affection. . . ." Deep in her heart, Mary knew that she was Shelley's "one great affection"—and tried hard to bide her time until the Godwins would take Claire back or some other solution might be found.

But Mary had other things on her mind besides the mundane problems of Shelley's financial worries, his legal difficulties with Harriet, and her own troubles with her family. There was the exalting life of the mind she shared with Shelley. There were books, art exhibitions, the theater to be shared. Mary was learning Greek, Latin, and Italian. Some days were pure bliss: "November 6th," Mary's diary reads. "Talk to Shelley. He writes a great heap of letters. Read part of *St. Leon* [a novel by Godwin]. . . . this is a day devoted to love in idleness. Go to sleep early in the evening." Most blissful of all, Mary was now preoccupied with the happiest task of her life, preparing for the birth of the baby she was now certain she was carrying!

Mary's days were full, although she wrestled with nausea constantly. How funny, she thought, that they called it "morning sickness"—when it went on all day! Still, she enjoyed this pregnancy—as she would all her later ones. In the first place, as a motherless child herself she was essentially a deeply lonely person, and the thought of a helpless infant who would turn to her for love was profoundly comforting. Then, too, Mary had a well-developed life of the mind; the very physical side of pregnancy and nurturing a baby made her feel like a balanced woman—a sort of "earth mother."

Being a mother-to-be was best when her days also included the intellectual work that was so familiar a part of her life. Under Shelley's encouragement she set a heavy writing schedule. She began an extended work which she called *The Life of Louvet*, and that took her mind off her queasy stomach and the chaos of the people around her. "Write in the morning," reads her diary of November 13.

> Very unwell all day. Fanny sends a letter to Claire to come to Blackfriars Road; Claire cannot go. Fanny comes here; she will not see me; hear everything she says, however. They think my letter cold and indelicate. . . . Papa tells Fanny if she sees me he will never speak to her again. . . . Fanny goes back to Skinner Street to get some [clothes]. She returns; Claire goes with her. Shelley returns . . . he disapproves. Write and read. In the evening talk with my love about a great many things. . . . Very unwell in the evening.

While Mary was preoccupied with her pregnancy, word came that Harriet had already delivered a son, Charles, a month prematurely, on November 30. Mary felt bitter. *Her* child would be illegitimate, and the birth of Shelley's "rightful" son and heir reminded her of what she tried so hard to forget: The man she loved had other legal ties. "A letter from Hookham, to say that Harriet had been brought to bed of a son and heir," she wrote in her diary. "Shelley writes a number of circular letters of this event, which ought to be ushered in with ringing of bells, &, for it is the son of his *wife.*" The same day a letter came from Harriet; Mary scornfully recorded the signature, underlining it: "from a *deserted* wife." Mary was too young, too oppressed by her own physical and emotional pressures, to want to understand Harriet's.

The birth of his legitimate baby was in some ways

a relief to Shelley, Mary knew. It secured to his line the succession of title and entitled estates, a financial benefit that was realized after the death of Shelley's grandfather, Sir Bysshe, a little more than a month later. Shelley met with his estranged father to settle their affairs, and although there was no narrowing of the breach between them—like Godwin, Sir Timothy could not forgive his offspring for an "illicit romance"—Shelley and his father came to an agreement that materially bettered Shelley's position. By June 1815 matters seemed settled; Shelley was to get one thousand pounds a year, of which he promptly assigned Harriet two hundred.

If it had not been for Godwin's continued bleeding of their funds—and Shelley's wrong-headed compulsion to mortgage his inheritance by supporting Godwin—Mary and Shelley might have escaped a life of picturesque poverty. As it was, the money did little good. Godwin immediately relieved Shelley of three thousand pounds, and Mary and Shelley continued to live in "lodgings" and worry about debtors.

The last few months of strain and excitement told sadly on Mary's health. For all her courage and will, she was somewhat frail physically. Although she yearned for a baby, her young body was not strong enough to carry a child to full term. On February 22, she awakened in pain. The baby was not due for two months, she reasoned, and resolutely she decided to go on as usual. By afternoon though, there was no use in ignoring the signs and a doctor was sent for. Shelley's diary records the birth—and its sad outlook: "[Mary] is in labour, and, after a few additional pains, she is delivered of a female child; five minutes afterwards Dr. Clarke comes; all is well. [Mary] perfectly well, and at ease. The child is not quite seven months; the child not expected to live."

Mary fell in love with the tiny little girl at once. No matter what the doctor said, the baby would live! Mary willed herself to regain her strength. "Mary quite well; the child, unexpectedly, alive, but still not expected to live," Shelley wrote the next day; tentatively on February 24, "Mary still well; favourable symptoms in the child; we may indulge some hope." Finally, miraculously, on February 25: "The child very well; Mary very well also."

Mary was overjoyed. She got out of bed, began to take over the care of the baby and the household. Happily the Godwins were away, and Fanny was able to come over and stay the night. Fanny, an aunt for the first time, was as adoring as Mary, and Mary was able to bask in the glow of having a sympathetic *woman* to "mother" her when she was tired and share her happiness as the baby began to grow pink-cheeked and healthy. Together they sent Shelley and Claire out to buy a cradle, while they settled back to the closeness they had known when they were two motherless girls in a lonely, unloving home.

Two weeks later the tragedy came. Just what happened remains a mystery. Mary's stark entry in her diary reads only: "Monday, March 6. Find my baby dead. Send for Hogg. Talk. A miserable day." The letter calling for Hogg tells a little more: "My dearest Hogg my baby is dead," reads the heartbreaking little missive—

will you come to me as soon as you can—I wish to see you—It was perfectly well when I went to bed—I awoke in the night to give it suck it appeared to be *sleeping* so quietly that I would not awake it. It was dead then, but we did not find *that* out till morning—from its appearance it evidently died of convulsions—

Will you come—you are so calm a creature & Shelley is afraid of a fever from the milk—for I am no longer a mother now Mary

Hogg was indeed her friend and her comfort. In her misery, Mary put out of her mind the truth—Shelley, whom she loved with all her heart, was preoccupied with himself. His genius was a demanding taskmaster, and although he wanted to make Mary happy, his own inner voices often drowned out her pleas for help. Mary began the pattern she was to follow during all their years together: to keep her sorrows to herself, to throw herself into reading, writing, intellectual pursuits, to distract herself from the intermittent heartbreak of her life, and even finally, in her blackest moments, a retreat so completely into herself that she would spend long periods alone, unable even to talk.

Mary's curt entries in her diary during this period show the valiant efforts she made at self-control:

Wednesday, Mar. 8— Finish "Rinaldini." Talk with Shelley. in very bad spirits, but get better; sleep a little in the day. In the evening . . . Hogg comes; he goes at half-past 11. Claire has written for Fanny, but she does not come.

Thursday, Mar. 9 Read and talk. Still think about my little baby—tis hard, indeed, for a mother to lose a child. Hogg and Charles Clairmont come in the evening—Read Fontenelle, "Plurality of Worlds."

Monday, Mar. 13. Shelley and Claire go to town. Stay at home . . . and think of my little dead baby. This is foolish, I suppose; yet, whenever I am left alone to my own thoughts, and do not read to divert them, they always come back to the same point—that I was a mother, and am so no longer. . . .

Sunday, Mar. 19— Dream that my little baby came to life again; that it had only been cold, and that we rubbed it before the fire, and it lived. Awake and find no baby. I think about the little thing all day.

But try as she might, Mary could not entirely banish the dark thoughts that haunted her after the baby's death. Perhaps a trip—a change of scene, always an escape for restless Shelley—might help, he thought, and sometime in May they set out on a tour in the west country.

The tour did the trick; Mary felt her spirits lightening at last. Besides, miracle of miracles, Claire decided to go off alone and live the rustic life in a Devonshire cottage. There she remained, at least for the time being, in a sort of "humourously tragic retirement," writing her usual charming, witty letters and scandalizing her country neighbors with her unconventional ways. Feeling that she and Shelley were at last free of any outside interference, Mary wrote jubilantly in her diary on May 13: "I begin a new journal with our regeneration."

The rebirth also took another direction. Mary's suspicions that she was again pregnant were confirmed by July. With another baby soon to be born, the couple thought it was a perfect time to settle down. They chose a house in Bishopsgate that was to be their first real home.

Mary's diary proved to be prophetic. This *was* the summer of their regeneration—an almost magical time for her. The hard times of the past year had drawn them closer together, Mary thought, had added depth to their passion. Shelley told her so in a thousand ways—most important to her, through his work. She had brought him strength and maturity; he soared ahead to write his superb poem *Alastor*, in which he describes his self-development through his love for Mary. "His mind is at length suddenly awakened and thirsts for intercourse with an intelligence similar to itself," he wrote in the poem's preface. "He imagines to himself the Being whom he loves."

The summer drifted by as peacefully as the river on which they spent many lazy afternoons. In August, they planned a boating excursion. Charles Clairmont, who went along, records that they spent a day at Oxford—in the rooms "where the two noted infidels, Shelley and Hogg (now, happily, excluded from the society of the present residents), pored, with the incessant and unwearied application of the alchymist, over the certified and natural boundaries of human knowledge." Mary watched contentedly as Shelley grew happier and more robust. She quite agreed with

Charles when he wrote: "We have all felt the good effects of this jaunt, but in Shelley the change is quite remarkable; he has now the ruddy, healthy complexion of the autumn upon his countenance, and he is twice as fat as he used to be."

Watching the summer unfold, Mary was serene and tranquil. Her pregnancy was comfortable—none of the wretched morning sickness that had marred her first. She felt, along with Shelley, that the calm wind of their contentment had ". . . swept from the wide atmosphere/Each vapour that obscured the sunset's rays."

By the end of the year, however, clouds were on the horizon again. Harriet and her family sought custody of her two children—Ianthe and Charles—and Shelley took the matter to court. Shelley turned to his father for help, but Sir Timothy, as always guided by the worry about "what people will think," thought it best for Shelley's children to be brought up in a more conventional atmosphere than Shelley's influence would make. Instead, he started further litigation over the family estate to prevent Shelley from burdening it with debts.

Debt was still the major problem, and at its core was the intractable figure of Godwin. A vicious rumor had been afloat for some time: Gossip said that Godwin had *sold* Mary and Claire to the poet! Mary and Shelley were outraged about the slander, but they felt guilty too, for if they had not run away together, the filthy rumor would never have come about. To salve their consciences—and because Mary was still attached to her brilliant and difficult parent—Shelley continued to fulfill what he considered his duty to the older man. In return, Godwin wrote to Shelley in the most bitter terms. His disapproval remained as strong as when he had told Shelley in 1814,

> I could not have believed that you would sacrifice your own character, and usefulness, the happiness of an innocent and meritorious wife, and the fair and spotless fame of my young child, to passion—I could not believe you wd. enter my house under the name of benefactor, to leave behind an endless poison to corrode my soul.

As an antidote to that "poison," Shelley continued to mortgage his income and Mary's security.

The one bright spot in Mary's life that autumn was that Claire was absent. Furthermore, her letters were strangely mysterious, and for the first time since they had all gone off together, Mary felt no responsibility for Claire. Whatever Claire was doing, she intended to keep it apart from Mary and Shelley!

Claire was, in fact, up to an unusual amount of mischief, even given her talents for getting into trouble. For years she had lived under the shadow of real genius—Godwin's, Mary's, and now Shelley's. Because of the accident of her mother's marriage, she had been thrust into a luminous society to which her own sparse abilities never would have given her entry. She had chafed for years under a sense of inferiority. Now she was determined to assert herself in some spectacular way.

The opportunity soon presented itself. Lord Byron, the most dashing and surely one of the handsomest men in England, was then connected with the Drury Lane Theatre. Claire dressed up in her most flamboyant costume and took herself to the playhouse. She wanted to become an actress, she told Byron. The infamous poet, bored and restless, responded half-heartedly to her flirtatious ways. "I was fain to take a little love (if pressed particularly) by way of novelty," he told his half-sister, Augusta. Claire pressed, and Byron soon had her with child.

Claire's pregnancy was a secret, not to be revealed for many months, but Mary's was drawing to a close. On the 24th of January, her baby was born. The little boy, whom they named William after her father, was a delight right from the beginning. A beautiful child, golden-haired and blue-eyed as Mary had been, he was bright, alert, a happy, healthy baby. Mary cooed over him, called him "Wilmouse"—her own name for herself in her playful love notes to Shelley was "Dormouse"—and spent endless hours daydreaming about his future. The little boy became the center of their household, and Mary, now eighteen, was every inch the doting mother.

But while Mary was content to stay at home with her baby—and always her reading and writing—Shelley, she saw, was once again becoming edgy. The solitude of being a new father did not agree with him. Shelley's temper was unusually short: He was feeling oppressed by Godwin. Shelley had no intention of hedging on what he saw as "obligation" to Godwin, but it was hard to be continually kind to a man who repaid you with nasty letters and harshness toward his own daughter! Shelley's friends, too, sensed the poet's mood: "The spirit of restlessness came over him," Peacock wrote. Mary began to cast about for a way of reviving Shelley's verve and enthusiasm. It soon came, once again in the presence of Mary's nemesis, Claire.

Claire had returned to the Shelley household full of ideas and schemes. Byron had lost interest in her almost immediately after they became lovers, but Claire was determined not to let him slip through her fingers. Her ace in the hole was Shelley.

Byron had more important matters on his mind than this lovesick conniving young woman who was becoming an albatross around his neck. His life, always a scandal, had erupted onto the front pages. Now his "domestic circumstances," whatever the gossip mongers of that time knew or pieced together about him, forced him into the decision to leave England forever. He drew together four friends, including his private physician, John Polidori, had a carriage made (it was copied from Napoleon's and had such features as a library and a chest of silverware), packed the unfinished manuscript of *Childe Harold's Pilgrimage*. Thus equipped, he embarked for Ostend, Flanders, the Rhine, and points south on April 25, 1816.

Claire kept the story of her brief affair and her pregnancy from Mary and Shelley. Slyly she made the suggestion: Wouldn't it be lovely, she asked, if Shelley and Byron were to meet? Shelley admired Byron's work, she knew, and here was the golden opportunity. If the three of them—Mary, Shelley, and Claire—were to go to the continent, who knew what might happen? The idea had enough appeal for Mary and Shelley to pack up their things—and baby William—and set off for Geneva in the first week of May.

The decision proved the second most important of Mary's life—overshadowed only by elopement with Shelley two years earlier. Then, the escape from her father's house catapulted her from adolescence to womanhood. Now, this journey to Switzerland abruptly ended her dreamy "scribbling" and day-dreaming, and thrust her into immortality as a writer. Everything she saw on the trip—the mountains and icy glaciers, the "pyramidal crags," cataracts, pine and chestnut forests, the scenes of "vast and dreadful isolation" she described in her diary—was material to be incorporated into her novel. The short stay on the shores of Lake Geneva put her under the intense stimulation of two of the most creative minds in Europe, Shelley and Byron, and that, too, was grist for her mill. Reaching back into her own childhood, searching around her in the world in which she lived—and in some inexplicable way looking ahead to life in the twentieth century—Mary, that summer, conceived the book that not only became a permanent addition to the world's literature of the macabre, but launched science fiction—*Frankenstein.*

5

Mary's Monster

Mary's Monster was conceived in what she called a "waking dream": "My imagination, unbidden, possessed and guided me, gifting the successive images that arose in my mind with a vividness far beyond the usual bounds of reverie." The Scientist and the Fiend are projections of Mary's unconscious mind—a storehouse of memories, images, emotions, thoughts, many of them unrecognizable to Mary in her conscious state but nevertheless born of her own life. In her story, all the characters are parts of Mary herself; the settings are created from the places she had seen or heard about; her characters speak in various familiar voices—Shelley's, Godwin's, and her own.

All of the lives Mary had lived in her eighteen years went into *Frankenstein*. There is Mary as a little girl, sitting in her father's study. There Godwin would talk to her about his theories of education, his belief that hereditary influences counted for nothing. Mary used this in creating her Monster, who was a "blank page" on which his own experiences and the people of his life would write good or evil, and so form him. Then there is Mary as an adolescent, crouching behind the sofa to listen to Coleridge read his poem *The Rime of the Ancient Mariner*. Mary used Coleridge's images to describe the mysterious white world of the ice-bound Arctic—Coleridge's "land of mist and snow"—as scenery for *Frankenstein*. There are even several references to the poem itself in the first chapters of her book—evidence of the impression that Coleridge's vision had on her when she was an eager, wide-eyed girl.

Much of the background that Mary drew from in *Frankenstein* came from places she and Shelley had visited together. She wrote about what they had seen during the first two years they lived with each other: storms in the Alps, the valleys of Servoz and Chamonix, the glacier and the steep sides of Montenvers, the "tremendous dome" of Mont Blanc, the thunder sounds of the avalanches and the great icy lakes of Switzerland.

Frankenstein is the story of the creation by a mortal of another living creature. This theme itself reflects Shelley's interest in the origins of life. *Frankenstein*, in fact, is subtitled "The Modern Prometheus" after the ancient myth that Mary based her story on and that Shelley himself was to use in his great poem *Prometheus Unbound*. Mary describes how her interest in the creation of life grew, in the introduction to the 1836 edition of her book:

Many and long were the conversations between Lord Byron and Shelley to which I was a devout but nearly silent listener. During one of these, various philosophical doctrines were discussed, and among others the nature of the principle of life, and whether there was any probability of its ever being discovered and communicated. They talked of the experiments of Dr. Darwin . . . who preserved a piece of vermicelli in a glass case till by some extraordinary means it began to move. . . .

Throughout the novel reference is made to science; indeed, Dr. Frankenstein himself is described as a chemist—all evidence of Shelley's contagious enthusiasm for the new study.

Most of all, though, the story is Mary's in its underlying motif of loneliness and solitude. There is Walton's solitary childhood, his lack of friends on board ship—all reflections of Mary's isolation as a child. The book tells how alone Mary felt through most of her life. The lonely laboratory, the hut on the "remotest of the Orkneys," the character of the Monster himself yearning for understanding and compassion, tell the tale of Mary, longing all her life for the love of her lost mother.

But underneath all the currents—philosophical, scientific, political, and social ideas—and its psychological aspect, *Frankenstein* is a horror story. It is a hair-raising, chilling story of terror that more than a century and a half after Mary put down her pen still has the power to fascinate, frighten, and haunt its reader. Here, sometimes in Mary's own words, are the outlines of the yarn she spun:

On the morning of December 11, 17—, an explorer named Robert Walton on his way to the North Pole posted a letter from St. Petersburg, Russia, to his sister, Margaret Sayville, back home in England:

"You will rejoice to hear that no disaster has accompanied the commencement of an enterprise which you have regarded with such evil forebodings," the letter began. Indeed, it continued, the writer was enjoying the cold northern breeze and the beauty and delight of the Arctic, where he hoped to discover the secret of the magnet. Ardent curiosity and the hope of a discovery that will bring benefit to humanity was his inspiration, Walton wrote. As for the difficulties? "What can stop the determined heart and resolved will of man?"

The evil forebodings were soon to come. Walton hired a boat, crewed it, and set off for the Arctic. There, on a frozen slab, surrounded by floating ice that closed in on the ship on all sides, many miles from land, he suddenly saw what he thought was an apparition. On one of the ice plains near the ship, a sledge drawn by dogs glided past. Guiding the dogs was what appeared to be a man—but of giant stature!

The next day Walton's sailors brought on board a man cast away on a floe, nearly frozen and emaciated by fatigue and suffering. Walton waited while the man slept and then had a hot meal. Finally the stranger recovered enough to explain why he had traveled so far on icy wastes. Sadly he replied to Walton's question: "To seek one who fled from me."

"And did the man whom you pursued travel in the same fashion?" Walton asked.

"Yes."

"Then I fancy we have seen him, for the day before we picked you up, we saw some dogs drawing a sledge, with a man in it, across the ice."

The stranger immediately sat up. "What route did the Demon take?" he asked.

Walton answered the questions as best he could. The stranger listened attentively. Then, encouraged by the stranger's interest, Walton began to speak about himself, his quest for knowledge, his desire to bring something back from the Arctic that would help humanity.

The stranger, now revealed as Dr. Victor Frankenstein, a Swiss scientist, interrupted Walton's monologue. "Unhappy man!" Dr. Frankenstein said brokenly. "Do you share my madness? Have you drunk also of the intoxicating draught? Hear me; let me reveal my tale, and you will dash the cup from your lips!"

After that outburst the traveler was too distraught to continue the conversation, but the next day, after a night's rest, he began to explain the chain of circumstances that had brought him there, to the edge of the Arctic.

Dr. Frankenstein was born in Switzerland, the son of an older devoted couple, he told his new friend. Other members of his family included his brother, William, seven years his junior, and a foster sister, Elizabeth, the beautiful and adored companion of all his childhood occupations. His closest boyhood friend was Henry Clerval, an imaginative and idealistic boy who dreamed of being a benefactor to mankind. Inspired by Clerval, young Victor became interested in science, read the books of the old alchemist Cornelius

Agrippa, and explored the world of nature in works by Albertus Magnus and Paracelsus.

But at the University of Geneva, where he went at seventeen to study science, Frankenstein learned from M. Kempe, his professor, that all his self-taught knowledge was wasted. "You have burdened your memory with exploded systems and useless names," M. Kempe told him. "In what desert land have you lived, where no one was kind enough to inform you that these fancies which you have so greedily imbibed are a thousand years old and as musty as they are ancient? My dear sir, you must begin your studies entirely anew."

The new studies led the young scholar directly to a professor of chemistry named M. Waldman. At that meeting his destiny was decided. "The ancient teachers of this science," the professor told Frankenstein,

promised impossibilities and performed nothing. The modern masters promise very little; they know that metals cannot be transmuted and that the elixir of life is a chimera. But these philosophers, whose hands seem only made to dabble in dirt, and their eyes to pore over the microscope or crucible, have indeed performed miracles. They penetrate into the recesses of nature and show how she works in her hiding places. They ascend into the heavens; they have discovered how the blood circulates, and the nature of the air we breathe. They have acquired new and almost unlimited powers; they can command the thunders of heaven, mimic the earthquake, and even mock the invisible world with its own shadows.

From that day on chemistry became Frankenstein's sole preoccupation. For two years he studied the science, and even invented some useful chemical instruments. Anatomy, too, fascinated him—the structure of the human frame, and the physiognomy of animals as well. Eventually he found his interest diverted to the great question of the origins of life itself. "Whence did the principle of life proceed?" he asked himself. Pondering, he decided that to examine life he would first have to study death. "I spent nights and days in vaults and charnel houses," he told Walton.

I saw how the fine form of man was degraded and wasted; I beheld the corruption of death succeed to the blooming cheek of life. I saw how the worm inherited the wonders of the eye and the brain. I paused, examining the change from life to death, and death to life, until in the midst of this darkness a sudden light broke in upon me—a light so brilliant and wondrous that I became dizzy with the immensity of the prospect which it illustrated.

Frankenstein had discovered the secret of giving life itself. He would make inanimate matter come alive!

Mad with his discovery, Frankenstein cast about for a way to use it. He would make a man, he decided, but what sort? At last he resolved to create a giant, about eight feet tall and proportionately large. This creature he would construct from parts of the bodies he would dig from graves.

"Who shall conceive the horrors of my secret toil as I dabbled among the unhallowed damps of the grave?" he asked Walton.

My limbs now tremble, and my eyes swim with remembrance. I collected bones from charnel houses. In a solitary cell at the top of my house, I kept my workshop of filthy creation. The dissecting room and the slaughter-house furnished many of my materials; and often did my human nature turn with loathing from my occupation as I brought my work near to a conclusion.

Then, at last, the job was done.

It was on a dreary night of November that I beheld the accomplishment of my toils [Frankenstein recounted]. With an anxiety that almost amounted to agony, I collected the instruments of life around me that I might infuse a spark of being into the lifeless thing that lay at my feet. It was already one in the morning, and my candle was nearly burnt out when, by the glimmer of the half-extinguished light, I saw the dull yellow eye of the creature open; it breathed hard, and a convulsive motion agitated its limbs.

The creature Frankenstein had created that seemed so beautiful to him now was revealed in all its monstrosity.

His yellow skin scarcely covered the work of muscles and arteries beneath; his hair was of a lustrous black and flowing; his teeth of a pearly whiteness, but these only formed a more horrid contrast with his watery eyes that seemed almost of the same colour as the dun-white sockets in which they were set, his shrivelled complexion and straight black lips.

Terrified, Frankenstein rushed out of the laboratory and into his bedroom where, after a long night spent pacing back and forth in despair, he at last flung himself on his bed and slept.

Sleep gave him no relief, for in his dreams he saw his foster sister Elizabeth turn into a corpse, his mother dead and in her shroud, worms crawling out of the flannel; and then, waking, he saw an even more horrible sight—the Monster itself, holding up the curtains of his bed, his eyes fixed on the scientist, his jaws moving, and inarticulate sounds escaping from between his grinning lips. Frankenstein, evading the hand that tried to detain him, fled downstairs to the courtyard to pass the rest of the night.

In the morning, scarcely aware of where he was going, he found himself walking into the village. A coach stopped and Henry Clerval, his boyhood chum, sprang out. "My dear Frankenstein," he exclaimed, "how fortunate you should be here at the moment of my alighting!"

Clerval's appearance was a happy distraction. He brought pleasant news about Frankenstein's father and brother, and about Elizabeth. It was not until he suggested returning to Frankenstein's college that the scientist remembered his Monster. Rushing upstairs, he looked into the laboratory and there, to his enormous relief, he found the room empty. Frankenstein clasped his hands with joy. His enemy had fled! Exultant, he ran down the stairs to join Clerval.

Dr. Frankenstein's obsession could not long be allayed. Fears and thoughts of his Monster kept crowding into his mind, and then, surrendering to his terror, he became ill. His brain fever kept him confined for several months, during which time he raved incessantly. Clerval's devoted nursing brought him slowly back to health and, at last, he was rational. As soon as he was recovered, Clerval handed him a letter from Elizabeth.

The note began, "You have been ill, very ill, and even the constant letters of dear kind Henry are not sufficient to reassure me on your account." It went on to bring happier news: Justine, a young girl whom the Frankenstein family had befriended some years earlier, had returned to the castle to work as a governess to William, his younger brother. William himself was thriving! "I wish you could see him; he is very tall for his age, with sweet laughing blue eyes, dark eyelashes and curling hair."

The letter cheered Frankenstein so much that within two weeks he felt recovered enough to leave his room. He took Clerval back to school with him to introduce his old friend to his professors. Clerval's interest in literature was a relief to Frankenstein, for he no longer wanted to discuss science. He longed to forget his experiment and the Monster he had created and lost. He and Clerval planned a vacation together to Germany, a trip that proved a complete pleasure and left him with lightened spirits and a return of his optimistic nature.

The mood was not to last long. A letter from his father awaited Frankenstein upon his return:

"I wish to prepare you for the woeful news. William is dead! That sweet child, whose smiles delighted and warmed my heart, who was so gentle, yet so gay! Victor, he is murdered."

Frankenstein hurried back to Geneva on his melancholy journey. The city was dark when he arrived, and he decided to visit the spot where his brother had been murdered. A storm came up and, standing in the gloom, Frankenstein felt the presence of a figure lurking in a clump of trees. Suddenly a flash of lightning illuminated the object and disclosed its shape, its gigantic stature, and the deformity of its appearance. Instantly he realized it was the wretch, the filthy Demon he had created. A terrible thought crossed his mind: It had been the Monster—the creature he had created—who had killed his brother!

The more Frankenstein thought about it, the more he was convinced that his horrible suspicion was correct. But when he arrived home, there was another explanation. The murderer had been found, his father told him. It was Justine, the young woman the family had befriended. The proof that she was guilty was that a locket she had stolen from little William that day was found later in her apron pocket.

Frankenstein wrestled with his conscience. He knew, somehow beyond doubt, who the real murderer was. But if he said nothing, surely Justine would be freed anyway. There was only circumstantial evidence, and certainly no jury would convict her. In the meantime, the tale of the Monster was not one to be announced publicly. Its astounding horror would be looked upon as madness, and nobody would believe him.

Frankenstein's gamble backfired. Innocent Justine was executed, and the scientist, overcome with conscience, escaped to seek solace in the mountains. There, on the glacier at Chamonix, he suddenly found himself face to face with the Monster.

Devil, [Frankenstein exclaimed], do you dare approach me? And do not you fear the fierce vengeance of my arm wreaked on your miserable head? Or rather stay, that I may trample you to dust. And oh! That I could, with the extinction of your miserable existence, restore those victims whom you have so diabolically murdered!

I expected this reception [said the Demon]. All men hate the wretched; how then must I be hated, who am miserable beyond all living things! Yet you, my creator, detest and spurn me. You propose to kill me. How dare you sport thus with life? Do your duty towards me, and I will do mine towards you and the rest of mankind.

The Monster then launched into his story—the tale of what had happened to him in the two years since Frankenstein had made him—and made a proposition to his creator.

"It is with considerable difficulty that I remember the original era of my being," the Monster began.

All the events of that period appear confused and indistinct. A strange multiplicity of sensations seized me. By degrees, a stronger light pressed on my nerves. Darkness then came over me and troubled me, but hardly had I felt this when, by opening my eyes, the light poured in on me again. I found I could wander on at liberty, and as I walked, I sought a place where I could receive shade. This was the forest near Ingolstadt; and here I rested until I felt tormented by hunger and thirst. I ate some berries which I found, slaked my thirst at the brook, and then lying down, was overcome by sleep.

Day by day his consciousness increased, the Monster continued. One day he found a fire and, enjoying its warmth, moved so close to it that he was burned. The next day he learned the fire's danger, how to control it, how to make a fire and use it for heat and light and to cook his crude food. One day, seeking food and shelter from the cold, he found a small hut. The door was open and the Monster entered the little cottage. Inside an old man sat near a fire, over which he was preparing breakfast. The old man turned, and seeing the Monster, he shrieked and fled. But the Monster, although bewildered, was not put off his hunt; he greedily devoured the remains of the shepherd's breakfast and then, overcome by fatigue, lay down on some straw and fell asleep.

The next morning he ventured farther—into a village. There, the vegetables in the gardens, the milk and cheese that he saw placed at the windows of some of the cottages, enticed him. He entered one of the huts, but hardly had he gone in before the children shrieked and one of the women fainted. The whole village was roused; some fled, others attacked him with stones. Bruised and frightened, he fled to the open country and took refuge in a deserted hovel. Thus protected from the elements—and the brutality of mankind—he arranged a home for himself.

The hovel was attached to a cottage and, from his hiding place, the Monster was soon able to observe the family who lived next door to him. By watching and listening, he learned human speech and taught himself to read. Listening to the trio—a young man, a beautiful girl, and an old man (apparently a father, a brother, and a sister)—he acquired a history of civilization. Happening on a suitcase full of books that included Plutarch's *Lives*, Milton's *Paradise Lost*, and Goethe's *The Sorrows of Werther*, he gained the elements of a classical and romantic education.

More important, though, to him was the growing love and admiration he felt for his neighbors. Their kind manners, their obvious devotion to each other, moved him, and he resolved to somehow make friends of these strangers. This resolve was strengthened by overhearing the family's own history: A combination of greed and corruption on the part of merchants, bankers, and government officials had reduced the family to exile and poverty.

Yet, having learned of the evils of society, the Monster still thought he had found future friends in his neighbors. His first encounter supported this: He ventured into the cottage one day when the old man was alone. "Pardon this intrusion," the Monster began. "I am a traveller in want of a little rest; you would greatly oblige me if you would allow me to remain a few minutes before the fire."

The old man received him kindly and apologized for his blindness, which prevented him from offering the Monster food and drink. Then, while the Monster was basking in the old man's warm comradeship, the sister and brother unexpectedly returned. The girl, overcome by horror, fainted; and her brother sprang forward, pulled the Monster away from the old man to whom he was clinging for comfort, dashed the Fiend to the ground, and beat him violently with a stick. "I could have torn him limb from limb," the Monster recounted. "But my heart sank within me as with a bitter sickness, and I refrained. I quitted the cottage and, in the general tumult, escaped unperceived to my hovel."

Alone, the Monster reviewed his fate. There was none among men who would assist or aid him, he decided, and he could not love his enemies. "No, from that moment I declared everlasting war against the species and, more than all, against him who had formed me and sent me forth to this insupportable misery." The Monster's first act of vengeance was to burn the cottage belonging to the family he had loved. Then, traveling by night secure from the view of man, he set off on his search for Dr. Frankenstein, to seek comfort and even justice from the man who had created him.

The trip only reinforced his feelings of being an outcast—a creature with perceptions and passions who sought love but could invoke only hatred and fear in the eyes of others. Then, one afternoon as he was asleep in a glen, he awakened to the sound of a child's footsteps. Suddenly an idea seized him. The little boy was too unprejudiced and had lived too short a time to have learned a horror of deformity, he thought. The Monster would seize him, educate him to be a companion, and in so doing no longer be desolate and alone upon the earth!

The Monster came out of his hiding place and put his arms around the child. The boy screamed in terror. "Child," the Monster remonstrated, "what is the meaning of this? I do not intend to hurt you; listen to me."

The boy struggled violently. "Let me go," he cried. "Monster! Ugly wretch! You wish to eat me or tear me to pieces. You are an ogre. Let me go or I will tell my papa."

"Boy, you will never see your father again; you must come with me."

"Hideous monster! Let me go. My papa is a syndic—he is M. Frankenstein—he will punish you. You dare not keep me."

"Frankenstein! You belong then to my enemy—to him towards whom I have sworn eternal revenge: you shall be my first victim."

The child struggled; the Monster grasped him by the throat and in a moment the boy lay dead at his feet. "I too can create desolation," the Monster exulted. "My enemy is not invulnerable; this death will carry despair to him, and a thousand other miseries shall torment and destroy him."

As the Monster stared at the small body of his first victim, he saw a locket—the porcelain miniature of the boy's mother. He took it from the boy's clothes and put it in his pocket. Then, seeking a hiding place, he came upon a barn. Inside, Justine was asleep, her beautiful face peaceful and serene. The Monster bent over her, thought about being loved by a woman such as this, and then with mounting bitterness realized it would never be. Vengeful again, he placed the locket he had taken from the child in the folds of the girl's dress. "Not I, but she shall suffer," he told himself. "The murder I have committed because I am forever robbed of all that she could give me, she shall atone."

The Monster, now having completed the terrible story of his crimes, turned again to Dr. Frankenstein to make his proposal. "I am alone and miserable; man will not associate with me; but one as deformed and horrible as myself would not deny herself to me. My companion must be of the same species and have the same defects. This being you must create!"

Dr. Frankenstein's first response was horror and hatred for the murderer of his brother. "I refuse," he cried. "No torture shall ever extort a consent from me. Shall I create another like yourself whose joint wickedness might desecrate the world? Begone! I have answered you."

"You are in the wrong," replied the Fiend. "I am malicious because I am miserable. Am I not shunned by all mankind?" The Monster continued in this vein beseechingly.

What I ask of you is reasonable and moderate. I demand a creature of another sex, but as hideous as myself. It is true, we shall be monsters, cut off from all the world; but on that account we shall be more attached to one another. I swear, by the sun and by the blue sky of heaven, that if you grant my prayer, you shall never behold me again.

Dr. Frankenstein was torn by two emotions—a sense of justice and a fear that if he refused the Monster would be roused to further destruction. Reluctantly, he agreed. He made plans to retreat to a solitary place, the remote Orkney Islands, where unseen and unknown he could create a mate for his Monster.

The months of creation went by slowly—all the more so because during his visit at home Dr. Frankenstein had acquiesced to his father's request that he set a date for his wedding to his beloved Elizabeth. Now, with Elizabeth waiting at home for him, and the promise of a new life with her, his work on the Monster's mate seemed interminable. More than that, the work was detestable. During his first experiment, a kind of enthusiastic frenzy had blinded him to the horror of his job, but now he was forced to work in cold blood. Terrible questions were always in his mind: The Monster had promised to hide in deserts, never to threaten humanity again, but suppose those terms were not agreeable to his mate? Suppose they were to have offspring, create a race of hideous monsters? Finally, his path seemed clear. He must destroy the new being he was creating; his Monster must not have a bride.

Feverishly Dr. Frankenstein set about the task, but no sooner had he completed it than he saw in the moonlight the Monster's face at the window of his laboratory. The Monster had followed him, had loitered in forests and caves, and now had come to claim the promised mate.

The door opened and the Monster confronted Dr. Frankenstein. "You have destroyed the work you intended, you have broken your promise."

"Begone! I do break my promise; never will I create another like you, equal in deformity and wickedness."

The Monster's retort was,

Slave, I believe I reasoned with you, but you have proved yourself unworthy of my condescension. Remember that I have power; you believe yourself miserable, but I can make you so wretched that the light of day will be hateful to you. You are my creator, but I am your master. Obey!

But Frankenstein was resolute. "Devil, cease. Leave me; I am inexorable."

"It is well. I go; but remember, I shall be with you on your wedding night."

Long after the Monster escaped from the house into the dark woods, his words rang in Dr. Frankenstein's ears. *I shall be with you on your wedding night.* But the next manifestation of the Monster's revenge was neither Elizabeth nor Dr. Frankenstein himself. It was Clerval, whose murdered body was found near the place Frankenstein had agreed to meet him. The murder seemed unsolvable and Frankenstein himself the main suspect—a situation that caused the doctor's imprisonment for three months. Finally, the case came to trial and Dr. Frankenstein was able to prove that he was elsewhere at the time of the murder.

Free once again, the scientist resumed his journey home to Geneva. In Paris a letter from Elizabeth awaited him. It spoke of their plans for marriage. Dr. Frankenstein was racked with indecision. The Monster's threat he interpreted to mean the murder of himself. Should he go ahead with a wedding that might make Elizabeth a widow so swiftly? At last he resolved his doubts. Life was unbearable to him —why not at least fulfill his promise to Elizabeth and to his father? "I fear, my beloved girl," he wrote in answer, "little happiness remains for us on earth; yet all that I may one day enjoy is centered in you. I will confide this tale of misery and terror to you the day after our marriage. But until then, I conjure you, do not mention or allude to it."

Dr. Frankenstein never had the chance to confide in Elizabeth. On the night they were married he nearly told her. Then, deciding to postpone it, he returned her to her room in the castle. Suddenly a shrill and dreadful scream pierced the air. It came from Elizabeth's room. He rushed into her chamber. There, lifeless and inanimate, thrown across the bed, her hair hanging down and her pale and distorted features half covered by her hair, lay the corpse of his bride. Hanging over her in an agony of despair, the scientist happened to look up. The window shutter had been opened, and there in the moonlight he saw the hideous figure of the Monster, a grin on the creature's face, jeeringly pointing his finger at Elizabeth's body. The scientist rushed toward the window, drew a pistol from his shirt, and fired, but the Monster eluded him and, running with the swiftness of lightning, plunged into the lake.

The scientist's course was decided. For the next few days he mourned his loss and then he paid a last visit to the graveyard in which Elizabeth was buried. Kneeling on the grass he pledged:

I swear to pursue the demon who caused this misery until he or I shall perish in mortal conflict. I call on you, the spirits of the dead, to aid and conduct me in my work. Let the cursed and hellish monster drink deep of agony; let him feel the despair that now torments me.

Dr. Frankenstein set off on the journey that ultimately led him to Walton's ship. In pursuit of the Monster he followed the windings of the Rhone River. Through the frozen forests of Russia Frankenstein followed the Monster's tracks. Now and again he would see the print of huge steps on the white plain. Sometimes the Fiend left marks in writing on the bark of trees or cut in stone that guided him and instigated his fury. "My reign is not yet over" were the words of one inscription. "You live, and my power is complete. Follow me. I seek the everlasting ices of the north, where you will feel the misery of cold and frost," read another. "Come on my enemy; we have yet to wrestle for our lives, but many hard and miserable hours must you endure until that period shall arrive."

The Monster's spoor led Frankenstein to the Arctic itself. He obtained a sledge and dogs. Driving the sledge with increasing urgency, Frankenstein would now and again catch sight of the Monster, always leading him on, always taunting him. Then, when he seemed almost in grasp of his foe, a tumultuous sea rose and he was cast on an ice floe—the refuge he had found when Walton rescued him.

But Walton's ship proved finally to be no haven for Dr. Frankenstein. The ship itself was soon in trouble, threatened by giant icebergs and in danger of being destroyed unless Walton turned south, away from his destination. While Walton was torn between his crew, who urged him at risk of mutiny to abandon his journey, and his own determination to proceed to the Pole, Frankenstein sickened. With his final strength, he called Walton to fulfill the scientist's unfinished work: "Oh, Walton," he pleaded, in a fit of enthusiastic madness I created a rational creature and was bound to assure his happiness. I refused to make him a mate; I felt a greater loyalty to beings of my own species. The fiend showed unparalleled selfishness in evil; he destroyed my friends. That he may render no other wretched, he ought to die!

Frankenstein's death that night left Walton shaken and sorrowful. He went into his room to write a letter to his sister. Suddenly he heard a sound—it was like a human voice, but hoarser, coming from the cabin in which Frankenstein's body lay. There, hanging over the corpse of his maker, was the Monster, his hideous face twisted with grief. "This is also my victim," the Monster exclaimed.

In his murder my crimes are consummated. Oh, Frankenstein! Generous and self-devoted being! What does it avail that I now ask thee to pardon me? I, who irretrievably destroyed thee by destroying all thou lovedst. Alas! He is cold, he cannot answer me.

"Your repentance," Walton told him, "is now superfluous. It is not pity you feel; you lament only because the victim of your evilness is now beyond your power."

"Oh, it is not thus," the Monster interrupted.

You who call Frankenstein your friend seem to have a knowledge of my crimes and misfortunes. But am I to be thought the only criminal, when all humankind sinned against me? You hate me, but your abhorrence cannot equal that with which I regard myself.

Fear not that I shall be the instrument of future mischief. My work is nearly complete. I shall quit your vessel on the ice raft which brought me hither and shall seek the most northern extremity of the globe; I shall collect my funeral pile and consume to ashes this miserable frame. I shall no longer feel the agonies which now consume me or be the prey of feelings unsatisfied. I shall die, and what I now feel be no longer felt. Soon these burning miseries will be extinct. I shall ascend my funeral pile triumphantly and exult in the agony of the torturing flames. My spirit will sleep in peace. Farewell.

He sprang from the cabin window, as he said this, onto the ice raft which lay close to the vessel. He was soon borne away by the waves and lost in darkness and distance.

On this ambiguous note Mary ends her story, leaving the reader to decide whether the Monster means to destroy himself or to continue to wreak vengeance and murder on earth.

6

Mary's World

"There never was a wilder story imagined," said the *Edinburgh Review* shortly after *Frankenstein* appeared, speculating that the anonymous novel had probably been written by Shelley.

> Yet . . . it has an air of reality attached to it, by being connected with the favorite projects and passions of the times. The real events of the world have, in our day, too, been of so wondrous and gigantic a kind, the shiftings of the scenes in our stupendous drama have been so rapid and various, that Shakespeare himself, in his wildest flights, has been completely distanced by the eccentricities of actual existence.

"The eccentricities of actual existence" were the subject of other essays in the magazines that reviewed

Frankenstein. Blackwood's, which carried a review of *Frankenstein* written by Sir Walter Scott, also contained a history of the "Great Sea Serpent" and a description of a new moveable axle for carriages. *The Quarterly* gave an account of geographical exploration and discovery, including recent Russian voyages in the Arctic and in "Ancient and Modern Greenland," with the hint that "the ice offers many strange phenomena which deserve to be investigated by a philosophical observer." Other magazines spoke about social issues: the controversy over the Poor Laws, in which the question was whether or not the poor must be allowed to starve to death in order to decrease crime and take the pressure off overcrowded prisons. Mary's world was a place of cataclysmic social, political, scientific, and economic changes. Everything people had believed for centuries about religion, government, property, morals, knowledge, and education was being challenged.

Change—"the shiftings of the scenes . . . the eccentricities of actual existence"—was what Mary's world was all about. Some of the changes were almost unconscious. In 1791 an Italian physiologist named Luigi Galvani, in the course of some experiments on frogs, had noticed a correlation between muscle twitching and simultaneous contact with both iron and copper. He constructed a device of two different metals, placing one in contact with a frog's nerve, and the other with a muscle. The frog's leg twitched and jumped—the frog was "animated" against his will. Galvani had, of course, created an electric current. In 1746, Benjamin Franklin and three friends had built a simple apparatus and begun an exploration of electrical phenomena—culminating, finally, in his deceptively simple demonstration of flying a kite in a thunderstorm. Godwin's good friend Humphrey Davy, whose investigations of the composition of the oxides and acids of nitrogen sometimes took the form of experiments in Godwin's house in which literary friends like Coleridge inhaled nitrous oxide, or laughing gas, was doing breakthrough work investigating voltaic cells. Electricity, the power that was to move and illuminate the twentieth century, was, already in Mary's day, in its dawn age.

Scientific rationalization, the lush passions of the romantic imagination—all the paradoxical values of the age—swirled and eddied in Mary's homes, in her childhood memories of her father and his friends, in the home she made with Shelley. Mary spoke of it in her introduction to *Frankenstein*. "Invention," she wrote, "does not consist in creating out of void, but out of chaos. . . ." Some of the chaos was within Mary herself—her passionate romance with Shelley, her elopement, her conflicted love for her father, her joys and tragedies in motherhood. But equally important were the whirlwinds without: the substitution of science for superstition, democracy for monarchy, power machinery for human labor—all the changes in the eighteenth and nineteenth centuries to which our generation is the heir.

The Age of Science in which *Frankenstein* was set was a long time in coming. For centuries after the fall of Rome, the Western world looked backward. The Dark Ages left a long shadow over Europe: marauding invaders, feudal wars, serfdom, plagues, ignorance, and destruction. Religion and culture were centered in the monasteries, secular power in the hands of kings and barons of Teutonic descent. The questions raised by the Greeks—Plato's inquiry into the rational nature of man, Aristotle's "discovery" of the physical worlds of anatomy, biology, and botany—all were put aside. The ancient scientists sought formulas to turn lead into gold, magic potions to restore life. Albertus Magnus, in the thirteenth century, was said to have made an entire man of brass; Cornelius Agrippa, in the fifteenth century, dealt in spells and incantations, and in the sixteenth century Paracelsus, one of the prototypes of the Faust myth, attempted to create a homunculus, or "little man," out of sperm and horse manure.

The first stirrings of scientific and intellectual investigation, between the eleventh and thirteenth centuries, were centered in Florence and hardly touched England at all. But by the fifteenth century, the movement toward knowledge swept all Europe. The introduction of paper as a cheaper material than parchment brought a regular trade in manuscripts and, together with the invention of the printing press, made books available to scholars throughout Europe. The fall of Constantinople brought an emigration of scholars and a flood of manuscripts to the West. Nearly the whole of Greek literature, philosophy, and mathematics suddenly arrived in Italy. These timeless manuscripts opened medieval minds. Plato's visions of the nobler intuitions of the mind, Aristotle's common-sense insistence that people must trust their own senses for an understanding of reality, Pythagoras' and Euclid's mathematical formulas to explain the physical world in which we live, Ptolemy's scrutiny of the skies to explore the wonders of the universe beyond our own planet—all these cast doubt on the medieval notion that human destiny was entirely controlled by forces beyond human understanding.

The ideas fell on fertile ground. The all-powerful medieval church, with its hold on secular power and control of systems of thought, was weakened by internal strife. When an Augustinian friar named Martin Luther early in the sixteenth century put forth the idea that people did not need the intervention of "priests and kings," for "it belongs to each and every Christian to know and . . . judge doctrine. . . . The Bible belongs to all," the way was prepared for a reliance on individual conscience in making decisions about life and morality. After all, if salvation itself was within one's power, Luther said, what was not?

An Englishman named Sir Francis Bacon, who was born fifteen years after Luther's death, applied himself to the question of power. *Knowledge* is power, he decided—the mastery over the forces of nature by means of scientific investigation. People, he thought, ought to be neither like spiders, which spin things out of their own insides, nor like ants, which merely collect; but rather like bees, which both collect and construct. Discovering new ways of understanding the world around us and harnessing it to our needs required both a hypothesis and the orderly arrangement of data, but in order really to observe phenomena, people had to rid themselves of what he called "idols"—the old habits of seeing and thinking by rote.

Even while Bacon was framing his method of inductive reasoning—the process of drawing general conclusions from particular facts—other men who were better mathematicians than he had begun the first of a series of discoveries that would hurtle Europe into the modern age. The first of these geniuses, a fifteenth-century Pole named Nicolaus Copernicus, overturned the idea, so comforting to the medieval mind, that the earth was the center of the universe rather than an insignificant mass of matter spinning around a ball of fire called the sun. Copernicus' conclusions were based on a formula that made sense to the second of the supreme innovators, an Italian named Galileo Galilei, who lived a century later. But Galileo took Copernicus' work a step further. He had heard of a toy invented by a Dutchman named Leeuwenhoek—a telescope, which by the use of a lens fitted in a tube brought faraway objects near. Galileo knew enough optics to construct the instrument, and there before his very eyes was proof that Copernicus' deductions were correct!

Galileo's colleagues at the University of Padua thought his discoveries were witchcraft or sleight of hand; his "heretical ideas" brought him to the attention of the Inquisition and he was forced to "recant." Nevertheless, his discoveries, principally his "law of falling bodies," were borne out by Johannes Kepler, a German astronomer, and in turn prepared the way for the scientist who has been called the founder of modern physics, England's Sir Isaac Newton, who was born in 1642, the year Galileo died. Newton's laws of motion explained the moon's phases, the behavior of the planets and their satellites, the orbits of comets, and even the ebb and flow of the tides. The motion of inanimate objects—since the beginning of civilization the great mystery of life—was no longer thought to be caused by unknown forces. Now it was calculable and predictable by the use of mathematical formulas!

The mounting tides of discoveries in physics destroyed wide domains of medieval error in astronomy. So wonderful an instrument of knowledge—the use of experimental reasoning—could not be isolated to one field. Its methods could be used for all problems, as Newton himself suggested: investigations into the mysteries of our planet and even into exploration of the bodies and minds of people themselves.

A veritable explosion of scientific discoveries took place in the seventeenth century. Galileo first made serious use of the telescope for scientific purposes. He also invented the thermometer. It was his pupil Evangelista Torricelli who invented the barometer, in 1643. The air pump was invented by Otto von Guericke in 1650, and clocks, although not new, were greatly improved during this period. Using the new instruments and experimental methods, scientists plunged into unknown frontiers and came up with such advanced knowledge as William Gilbert's important work on the magnet in 1600 and William Harvey's discovery of the circulation of blood in 1628. Leeuwenhoek turned his attention from far-off distances to the microcosm as yet unseen. Using a microscope he built, he discovered protozoa and bacteria, and examined spermatozoa. Robert Boyle, a self-described "Baconian," investigated the nature of matter and laid the foundations for modern chemistry.

The boundaries of the Western world itself, too, were expanding, opening unknown continents to Europe. Columbus' bold venture into the West Indies persuaded the English King Henry VII, in 1497, to license John Cabot of Bristol to explore westward and "set our banners and ensigns in any town, city, castle, island or mainland whatsoever." Competition for the prize—the untold riches of the Americas—led to a battle for dominion over the seas, with England finally the victor.

The plundered wealth of the Americas flooded Europe. England began the changeover from an agrarian economy—in which people lived off the land—into a mercantile one, with money and power now shifting from landlords to bankers and traders, merchants and shipowners. New fortunes sprang up—a startling change in a society in which power had long rested in land and arms. This transfer of wealth and authority threatened kings and nobles who fought to maintain the old security of feudalism. Throughout Europe, the period from 1660 to the beginning of the nineteenth century was dominated by wars of religion and civil wars. Everywhere, there was a craving for freedom from the old restrictions, for equality among people—a yearning that was to shape the new century.

Men and women at the eighteenth centennial—the end of the century in which Mary Shelley was born—had many reasons for self-satisfaction. Europeans had looked to the skies and discovered a new astronomy. They had looked into the world around them and, in Mary's words, "penetrated its mysteries." They had, indeed, become lords of all the world. They had conquered North and South America, they were powerful in Africa and India, respected in China, feared in Japan. They were no longer "miserable sinners," helpless in the face of blind forces that controlled their destinies. They were no longer ignorant and unlettered; at least among the upper classes there was widespread literacy and books were easily available. They were no longer under the thrall of feudal barons or medieval priestcraft.

Still, a burning question persisted. How were people to harness all the knowledge, power, and wealth they now possessed in ways that would make life here on earth the paradise they felt they deserved? The debate began early in the century, and continued well into the next. Eventually, the pursuit of happiness came to be followed along one of two paths. The first philosophy was pragmatic, utilitarian, devoted to the idea of the "greatest good for the greatest number of people." The second way was romantic, passionate, devoted to the concept of the rights of the individual. In Mary's lifetime, Godwin was the disciple of the first concept, while Byron was the prophet of the second, and in Mary's book *Frankenstein* the two philosophies overlap and blend.

English utilitarians believed that humanity's salvation was in science, not in sacrament. Through the intellect, not through the emotions, humankind could remold the world, adjust the environment to meet human needs. Utopia was within reach. Modern industry, then in its dawn age, was one key—for clearly people had the means to produce without hard toil all the goods they needed. Democracy was another. Challenges to the concept of the "divine right" of kings eroded absolute monarchy in England. When, in the mid-seventeenth century, conflict over religious and constitutional issues led to an open break between king and Parliament, Parliament won and beheaded the king. The Glorious Revolution of 1688 finally broke the power of the English monarchy, and set into motion the forces that inevitably introduced the basic tenets of modern democracy: Government is a matter of contract between equals, rather than a hierarchy established by birth.

The first of the utilitarians—the theorist whose ideas link the English Revolution of 1688 and the American and French Revolutions at the end of the eighteenth century—was an English physician named John Locke. In his *Essay Concerning Human Understanding,* which he finished in 1690, and particularly in his *Two Treatises on Civil Government* (also 1690), he outlined the principles that found their way—nearly verbatim—into both the Declaration of Independence and the Constitution of the United States: the inalienable rights of the individual; the civil contract as an affair purely of this world, not something established by divine right; a system of checks and balances to insure that power would always be controlled. In America, Locke's most prominent disciple was Mary Wollstonecraft's friend Thomas Paine; in France it was a brilliant writer and philosopher named François Voltaire, and in England it was Godwin.

Godwin's principles were firmly established by the time Mary was born. He had, indeed, spelled them out clearly in his major books, *Political Justice* and *Caleb Williams,* both published a few years before Mary's birth. Basically, Godwin laid the blame for people's unhappiness on the institutions under which he thought they lived—a repressive government and an authoritarian religion. People, though, he thought could change, become "perfect," mold society to fit their needs. He did not believe in hereditary differences: Change a nobleman's child with a peasant's and each will grow up quite naturally in his new life. "Nature never made a dunce," Godwin wrote. It was school that slaughtered the mind. Vice was an error—not a sin. His belief about punishment was that it didn't work. Along with Socrates, he asked the question: "Do you punish a man to make him better or worse?" If you point out to a person the error of his ways, Godwin thought, he would naturally want to reform.

Godwin thought everybody should share in the wealth of the earth, but he didn't believe in violent revolution. As soon as private ownership was seen as only greed, there would be a revolution in *opinion*. Selfishness would vanish and people would help each other. They would stop doing unnecessary work: Godwin thought that two hours of labor a day would be enough to produce all the necessities of life, since modern machinery could be developed to do all the menial tasks. People would then be free for study and the higher life.

But even while theorists like Godwin were viewing science and rational thinking as the swords to cut down all the evils of the past, another group of philosophers and writers had begun to focus on the dark side of the modern age.

The Industrial Revolution—the substitution of power-driven machinery for human toil, the very means by which Godwin thought people could build Utopias—was already proving a mixed blessing. A swift proliferation of inventions in the last half of the eighteenth century—James Hargreaves' spinning jenny in 1764, Edmund Cartwright's power loom in 1785, James Watt's steam engine in 1765 among them—changed the economy and reached right down into the lives of the people themselves.

Where once England had been a land of pastoral villages, there were now huge factories and squalid tenements. A new army of wage slaves—men, women, and children—would leave their homes each day to take their places behind flying shuttles, water frames, and power looms. Workers labored long hours for small wages in huge, impersonal factories. With no labor legislation to regulate hours and wages, no welfare or social security to take over when wage earners could not work, no unemployment benefits when they were laid off, working people were at the mercy of conditions they could not control.

Against these stark realities there emerged the second of two dominant systems of thought in the eighteenth and nineteenth centuries—Romanticism. The Romantics began by asking these questions: Is this what humanity was created for—to become faceless cogs in a huge machine, to work in mechanized factories, to live in cramped, windowless cells, away from the beauty of the universe and the majesty of nature? Surely, they decided, salvation was in a return to simplicity, to the earth itself, in the words of Jean Jacques Rousseau, the Swiss-born French writer who was the principal figure in the movement, to humanity in its natural state, to the "noble savage."

Rousseau's ideas about the modern world were summed up in his *Discourse on the Origin of Inequality*, which he wrote in 1754. "That men are actually wicked," he stated, "a sad and continual experience of them proves beyond doubt; but all the same, I think I have shown that man is naturally good. What then can have depraved him to such an extent, except . . . the advances he has made, and the knowledge he has acquired?" It is the fact that man possesses "the faculty for self-improvement," Rousseau continued, that "makes him a tyrant both over himself and over nature."

All "self-improvement" was bad, the Romantics thought, everything "natural" was good. They preferred man's innate nature to the one that was modified by education. They valued nature in its most primitive form—rugged mountains and primeval forests, the rural rather than the urban landscape. Emotions were "natural" and were highly prized, while intellect was decried. Most of all, the Romantics prized the rights of the individual to live a free and untrammeled life above the rights of society to sacrifice the specific to the general welfare.

Just as the utilitarian outlook lent itself to politics—to the redistribution of power and wealth—the Romantic movement lent itself to art. In painting and literature all things exotic, far-off, removed from modern civilization were admired: icy Arctic wastes, glaciers, waterfalls, tropical islands with lush flora and unfamiliar fauna and unspoiled "natives." Since distance lent enchantment—the distance of either time or space would do—antiquity was esteemed. Old castles, misty moors, ancient languages such as Old Norse, Old English, and the Celtic tongues, a revival of chivalry and Elizabethan drama, all were symbols of the Romantic imagination.

Romanticism took form in prose in Edmund

Burke's essay "The Sublime and Beautiful," in which the author distinguishes between beauty founded on pleasure, and therefore is placid, and the sublime, which inspires awe and terror. In poetry, Romanticism emerges in the early work of William Wordsworth, to whom the later Romantic poets Shelley, Byron, and Keats looked for inspiration, and in Coleridge's *Rime of the Ancient Mariner*. In fiction, Romanticism fostered the "Gothic novel," with its emphasis on the distant and unearthly. In this genre, the most representative was Matthew Lewis' *The Monk*, a novel overloaded with romantic robbers, ghosts, a bleeding nun and an evil monk, murder, torture, and matricide. It was, in fact, the book that Mary, Shelley, and Byron all read that summer in Switzerland that *Frankenstein* was begun.

The Romantic mood permeated even science, chiefly in the figure of Dr. Erasmus Darwin, a remarkable man who was part of the Godwin circle, and to whom Mary gives credit in the inspiration of *Frankenstein*.

Speculations on the origins of life were current at the end of the eighteenth century. The ancient Greeks had held advanced views on evolution and natural selection; Thales believed that water is the basic element of all things, and Anaximander believed there was a primary substance through the separation of which all things were created. But for centuries the Judeo-Christian belief in the origin of life, as described in the Bible, had halted further inquiry. Then, in the early 1800's, the world of the South Seas, the first region of the globe to be opened to the West scientifically, was explored and yielded strange variations in life forms. These discoveries raised anew the old questions about how our planet, its animals, and people came about.

The most colorful of the scientists who looked to solve these enigmas was Erasmus Darwin, one of Godwin's frequent visitors. Dr. Darwin was a physician by profession, a witty and forceful conversationalist, an inventor of such useful novelties as new types of carriages and coal cars, a speaking machine, a mechanical ferry, rotary pumps, and horizontal windmills. He also proposed a rocket motor powered by hydrogen and oxygen. His rough sketch shows a good approximation of the workings of a modern rocket—all put on paper a century and a half before missiles actually were to sail through the air!

But of all his achievements, the most notable contribution Darwin made was his mighty work *Zoonomia*, published in two volumes in 1794 and 1796. It is a precursor of *On the Origin of Species*, the book his grandson, Charles Darwin, was to publish in 1859. It is, moreover, the first work on the theory of evolution. Its arguments properly buttressed, the work actually began the long debate—not resolved for nearly a century—about whether the earth's inhabitants were created as fixed species, or whether life was in flux, all change. Erasmus Darwin's research postulates a theory of natural selection, the search for food, and the need for protection in living things, and how these factors control the diversity of life in all its changing forms.

This, then, was the world Mary lived in: a world of search for knowledge about the elements, energy, the changing forms of life itself—all the discovery, experimentation, the as yet undiscovered possibilities for humanity to modify the universe. But it must be remembered, too, that much of the world we now take for granted was completely unknown in Mary's time. Erasmus Darwin's theories had been published, but the general public was unaware of his novel approach—Charles Darwin was seven years old when *Frankenstein* was conceived. The fact that creatures such as dinosaurs once inhabited the earth was not known until ten years after Frankenstein's first roamings. Exploration of the Arctic, where so much of *Frankenstein* takes place, was fairly new, and explorers still searched for the Northwest Passage as late as the 1850's; the Antarctic was first sighted in 1819. Freud and psychology were almost a century away, and even socialist theory would not be introduced for another fifteen years. Germany and Italy were not yet countries, but clusters of little kingdoms; neither would be united for another half century.

So it is in the spirit of this search for knowledge that Mary's scientist, Dr. Frankenstein, explains:

> It was the secrets of the heaven and earth that I desired to learn, and whether it was the outward substance of things or the inner spirit of nature and the mysterious soul of man that occupied me, still my inquiries were directed to the metaphysical, or in its highest sense, the physical secrets of the world.

The times Mary lived in demanded nothing less!

7

"The Ups and Downs of This World"

It was almost as though the Monster scattered destruction in his wake—not only among the mountains and polar wastes he roamed, but even in Chapuis, the cottage in the Alps where Mary began his story.

The first rumble of trouble came in a letter from Fanny, Mary's half-sister, on August 9, 1816. It had been a routine day for Mary. She spent it writing *Frankenstein*, and later in the day reading. Shelley and Byron went boating on the lake, and Mary was glad to have the chance to work alone. But the letter was a disturbance, and when Shelley returned they discussed it.

The message was rambling. There was ordinary gossip and a bit of patter about library matters and politics. Then came the substance of the letter: "I left it to the end of my letter to call your attention most seriously to what I said in my last letter respecting Papa's affairs. They have now a much more serious and threatening aspect than when I last wrote to you." Godwin was deeply in debt, Fanny hinted; more than that, he was too involved with his own problems to notice Fanny's depression.

The next day Mary and Shelley bought Fanny a watch and sent it off to her. The little gift did not ease Mary's worries. Fanny was desolate, she knew. But Mary was busy with her writing, occupied with keeping a home and caring for a little baby, and having to deal with Claire's troubled romance as well. Besides, she was hundreds of miles away from Skinner Street. What could she do to help Fanny with what her half-sister called her "unhappy life"?

Resolutely, Mary decided to put Fanny out of her mind. Her days assumed a pattern of work—reading, writing, and sometimes in the evening excursions on the lake where she and Shelley drifted lazily around in a little boat, talking about themselves and each other and poetry and beauty. Sometimes she was invited to Diodati to spend the late evening with Byron, Shelley, and Polidori, and occasionally she joined in the conversations herself. One night she listened to an argument between Shelley and Byron about ghosts. Byron and his guest, "Monk" Lewis, the author of the gothic thriller about phantoms, demons, and haunted castles, scoffed at Shelley's "superstitions." Shelley argued that there was a world of the occult, not understood by reason. That night he wrote in his diary: "I do not think that all the persons who profess to discredit these visitations really discredit them." If they did, Shelley went on, it was only the *daylight*. At the approach of "loneliness and midnight," he continued, the skeptics were more likely to think "respectably" about "the world of shadows"!

But these evenings, as scary and entertaining as they were, and Mary's own disciplined approach to writing *Frankenstein*, did not completely block out her worries about what was going on at home. Although Mary had been given a nonconformist education, she was reared, like other girls of her time, with the idea that devotion to one's family came first. All her life the problems of others would rest heavily on her dutiful shoulders.

Actually, although Mary could not know it, Fanny was much worse off than she let on. Godwin had little time for his stepdaughter, and Mrs. Godwin offered the young woman no more love and understanding than she had given to Mary. Fanny felt like a burden to the household, unseen and unwanted. Her only hope was to leave Skinner Street and become independent. With that aim, she wrote to her aunts, Mary Wollstonecraft's sisters, to ask for a teaching position at the school they ran in Ireland.

Fanny eagerly awaited the arrival of the aunts who would offer what she missed at home—recognition and belonging. But the visit once again dashed her hopes. Her mother's sisters—whom Mary Wollstonecraft had sacrificed so much of her life to help—felt no obligation to their forlorn niece. Fanny was found unacceptable. The narrow-minded Wollstonecraft sisters decided that the girl had been "contaminated" by her sister's "irregular life," and left her again to her miserable existence in London.

Fanny was only one of Mary's concerns, as Mary,

Shelley, and Claire made preparations to return to England at the end of the summer. Claire's pregnancy was becoming more evident, and her condition would surely add weight to the ugly rumor circulating in England. Mary and Shelley knew that gossipmongers believed Shelley was living "in sin" with two women; Claire's baby, when it arrived, would surely be taken for Shelley's offspring! Once back in England, Mary took Claire and baby William to a hideaway in Bath, while Shelley went to stay with his friend Peacock to search for a house in which Mary, Claire, and the babies could live quietly and discreetly.

At the beginning of October, Mary managed to escape from Claire's increasing whining by joining Shelley for a few days alone at Marlow. Back at Bath, they were still lighthearted: One day Mary teased Shelley about "transfigurations." She poked her head into the office where Shelley was working and laughed: "Come and look. Here's a cat eating roses. She'll turn into a woman. When beasts eat roses they turn into men and women!"

The happy mood ended abruptly on October 9. A letter came from Fanny—this one truly alarming. It spelled out the girl's misery. Blow after blow had fallen, she wrote. She had lost Mary, her only bond with her mother. Now she had learned that Godwin, to whom she had devoted her short life, was not really her father! She had finally made the decision, she wrote heartbreakingly. She would "depart immediately to the spot from which I hope never to return."

The letter was postmarked Bristol. Shelley immediately hired a carriage and rushed off to find her—to stop her from what they knew was surely suicide.

Mary sat up until two o'clock in the morning, but Shelley returned alone and without any information about the missing girl.

The news came the following day. Fanny had gone to a room at an inn in Swansea, where she took her life. An empty laudanum bottle was found beside her, along with her last letter:

> I have long determined that the best thing I could do was to put an end to the existence of a being whose birth was unfortunate, and whose life has only been a series of pain to those persons who have hurt their health in endeavoring to promote her welfare. Perhaps to hear of my death will give you pain, but you will soon have the blessing of forgetting that such a creature existed as

Fanny, as ever the considerate daughter, in her last gesture omitted her name from her suicide note in order to protect Godwin's name. Godwin met the situation with dignified calm. "Go not to Swansea," he advised Mary,

> disturb not the silent dead; do nothing to destroy the obscurity she so much desired. . . . It was, as I said, her last wish; it was the motive that led her from London to Bristol and from Bristol to Swansea. . . .
>
> [D]o not expose us to those idle questions, which to a mind in anguish is one of the severest of all trials. . . .
>
> What I have most of all in horror is the public papers, and I thank you for your caution, as it might act on this. . . .

Our feelings are less tumultuous than deep.
God only knows what they may become. . . .

Mary followed his instructions and mourned Fanny
silently. She had to deal with her own remorse privately, because Shelley was so obviously agonized. He
was far more able to express his feelings openly—even
hysterically—than Mary. Always when he was in tur-
moil, he became physically ill. Mary worried about his
lungs—consumption was the "poet's disease," and
Shelley quickly lost the weight he had gained during
the previous summer and developed blue circles under
his eyes. Mary began at once to think about the solution so dear to both their hearts—a change of scenery.
"Sweet Elf," she wrote to him while he was on one of
his house-hunting absences,

> . . . in the choice of residence—dear Shelley—pray
> be not too quick or attach yourself too much to
> one spot— Ah—were you indeed a winged Elf
> and could soar over mountains & seas and could
> pounce on the little spot— A house with a lawn
> a river or lake—noble trees and divine mountains
> that should be our little mousehole to retire to.
> But never mind this—give me a garden & *absentia
> Clariae* [Claire's absence] and I will thank my love
> for many favours.

But Claire's absence was not remotely on the
scene. She was entering the last months of her
pregnancy. She felt ill, she complained, and needed
Mary's constant attention. Although Claire had
never been close to Fanny, her stepsister's death
made her more than usually hysterical. She had bad

dreams; she foretold gloom and tragedy again.

Claire's foreboding was not far wrong. The second mortal blow was about to fall. On December 14 Shelley returned to Bath, and on the following day the news came that Harriet, still his legal wife, had drowned herself in The Serpentine, a lake in London, five days before.

Mary had hardly known Harriet at all. While Fanny's suicide left her haunted with guilt, it would be years before she would feel any responsibility for Harriet's death. Now, she was still too caught up in her own jealousies and resentments: Harriet, she thought, had made everything so difficult for Shelley and herself. Mary did, however, have to deal with Shelley's emotions—and a strange mixture they were.

Shelley had long since lost his romantic passion for Harriet. To him, she was only a husk of the past. Her suicide, he thought, was almost inevitable—as early as 1811 he wrote that he had married her to save her from "this inertia at the bottom of her mind." Shelley could not think of love without rescue, and his opinion of Harriet was that "suicide was with her a favourite theme."

Besides Harriet's depressions—she had had them since childhood, and surely Shelley felt he was not responsible—there was another aspect to her character that freed him from guilt. Harriet was beautiful and flirtatious, and—rightfully or not—Shelley was convinced that she had been unfaithful. Shelley believed her to be pregnant by a lover at the time of her death, and it was not hard for him to lay her suicide on disappointment in love. Why, Shelley asked himself—and Mary—should *he* take the blame because his wife killed herself over another man?

But although Shelley felt no remorse at Harriet's death, he did feel pity. Harriet was only twenty-one when she died, and Shelley mourned the waste of her life. Harriet's premature death strengthened his resolve to rescue the two children he had with her, Charles and Ianthe, from Harriet's family. The Westbrooks—particularly Harriet's domineering sister, Eliza—would rear the children in the same atmosphere that had stifled Harriet, the conventional kind of home that had made Harriet unable to cope with life. Immediately after Harriet's death both Shelley and Mary set about to obtain custody of the two babies, while the Westbrooks just as promptly began litigation to prevent it.

There was no question in Mary's mind about her own loyalties. On December 17 she wrote to Shelley, who had gone to London to fight the Westbrook's suit:

My beloved friend,

I waited with the greatest anxiety for your letter— You are well and that assurance has restored some peace to me.

How very happy I shall be to possess those darling treasures that are yours . . . and wait with impatience for tomorrow when I shall hear whether they are with you. . . . My heart says bring them instantly here—but I submit to your prudence. . . .

These Westbrooks—But they have nothing to do with your sweet babes they are yours and I do not see the pretense for a suit but tomorrow I shall know all.

. . . I shall soon to the upholsterer—for now I long more than ever that our house should be quickly ready for the reception of those dear children whom I love so tenderly—then there will be a sweet brother and sister for my William who will lose his pre-eminence as eldest and be helped third at table,—as his Aunt Claire is continually reminding him.

While Mary was happily anticipating a home full of children to love, Shelley's lawyers called him into a conference. Shelley was now a widower, they reminded him, and he was free to marry Mary. The marriage, they told him, held a lot of advantages for him, for the courts would be much more likely to award custody of his children to him if he had a wife and a stable home. The poet thought it over and saw the logic of their argument, and then he went home to talk to Mary.

Mary agreed. She felt no need of a legal marriage herself—for she knew she was tied by stronger ties than mere legal ones, the bonds of love—but she was willing to go along with anything that would help Shelley regain his children. She wrote to him while he was in London seeing about the court case: "As to the event you allude to . . . it must be in London."

In London it was. Mary and Shelley were married on December 30, 1816, at St. Mildred's Church, in the presence of Godwin.

However unimportant the actual ceremony was to Mary and Shelley, it was "magical in its effects," as

Shelley said, in reconciling Mary and her father. The world's opinion, which once he had scorned, had now become necessary to Godwin's security. Overjoyed, he wrote the news to his brother:

> I went to church with this . . . girl some little time ago to be married. Her husband is the eldest son of Sir Timothy Shelley, of Field Place, in the county of Sussex, Baronet. So that, according to the vulgar ideas of the world, she is well married, and I have great hopes the young man will make her a good husband. You will wonder, I daresay, how a girl without a penny of fortune should meet with so good a match. But such are the ups and downs of this world. For my part I care but little, comparatively, about wealth, so that it should be her destiny in life to be respectable, virtuous and contented.

Mrs. Godwin, too, preened her own feathers as she let the word out about Mary's brilliant marriage. "I have now the pleasure to announce that Mr. Godwin's daughter, Mary, has entered the marriage state with Mr. Percy Bysshe Shelley, eldest son of Sir Timothy Shelley, Baronet . . ." she wrote to Archibald Constable, the publisher.

> We are now endeavoring to forget preceding sorrows, and to enjoy the flattering prospects which seem to present themselves. The young couple have been in town several weeks, principally under our roof, and my poor nerves begin to cry quarter from the bustle and feasting occasioned by the event.

Another event had come that Mrs. Godwin did *not* announce—the news was carefully kept from her. On January 13, 1817, her daughter Claire gave birth to Byron's child—a little girl whom she called Clare Alba, after Byron's nickname, Albe, but whom the poet renamed Allegra.

Mary's life was fuller than ever. Two babies to care for and love, Allegra and William, Shelley's struggles with courts and barristers to retain custody of his older children, her own writing—editing and transcribing the manuscript of Frankenstein—left her little time. But what there was of it, she devoted to the social life that was so dear to Shelley.

Shelley had missed his circle of friends in the early days of his romance with Mary. Like Mary, he needed time to write, read, and dream. But Shelley was a social creature—much more so than Mary, who was content to be alone with him and the children. He needed people with whom he could exchange ideas, read his poetry, share his literary life. Unlike Mary, who was a grown-up from the middle of her teens, Shelley had a lot of the little boy about him. He liked to sail paper boats on the lake, fly kites, set balloons aloft, cut up with his friends, play practical jokes. He had missed his companions; Hogg and Peacock, his old friends, had been cool for a time after he ran off with Mary, for Shelley's behavior shocked even the least conventional minds of his time, but they had gradually forgiven him and reestablished the intimacy.

Now Shelley found his circle once again growing. Some years before—in the spring of 1811, when he was nineteen—he had met the editor of *The Examiner*, a journal of literary quality and reputation, and he now resolved to submit a poem he had written in Switzerland, "Hymn to Intellectual Beauty," over the pseudonym "The Elfin Knight"—Mary's pet name for him. Leigh Hunt, the editor, didn't know who the Knight was, but he knew poetry when he saw it. He promised to publish the poem at the first opportunity. In the meantime, having seen more of Shelley's work, he identified him as the Elfin Knight and wrote a celebrated manifesto, "Young Poets," in which he honored Shelley, a twenty-five-year-old poet named John Keats, and John Hamilton Reynolds. These men, he foresaw, would shortly bring English poetry to a new life.

The association was not only splendid for Shelley's reputation, it also established a lifelong friendship between the Hunts and Shelleys. Though Shelley was discussed in the essay as an original thinker rather than a poet, he thought it was praise worth having. He immediately sent Hunt a check either for Hunt's use on *The Examiner* or to "help the distressed poor at Spitalfields," and arranged to meet Hunt himself at Hampstead. "I have not in all my intercourse with mankind experienced sympathy and kindness with which I have been so affected or which my whole being has so sprung forward to meet and to return. . . . Let me talk with you as with an old friend," Shelley wrote to Hunt.

Old friends they shortly became. Shelley brought Mary to Hunt's cottage—the Vale of Health—and Mary and Marianne Hunt took to each other immediately. The Vale of Health was always filled with people—bubbling Marianne and her five lively children, and a collection of people of genius and those who honored genius. The Shelleys felt tied to the Hunts and their distinguished friends by a regard for free beauty in life, literature, music, and the fine arts.

At the Hunts', the Shelleys met the literary lions of England—William Hazlitt and John Keats among them. Shelley was excited at the thought of being introduced to Keats, but the meeting was a disappointment. Keats was the son of middle-class parents, and he was stiffly uncomfortable with the high-born Shelley. Shelley's honest appreciation of Keats' formidable talent did not ease the encounter; Keats, who generally was a warm and friendly young man, vastly popular, retreated into a shy aloofness that Shelley could not break down.

Still, the Shelleys' social life bloomed, and in order to accommodate the family and the burgeoning circle of friends, they took a lovely old house at Marlow. They immediately filled it with books and people. Mary wrote a hospitable letter inviting the Hunts for a long visit: "Our house," she wrote temptingly,

> is very political as well as poetical and I hope you will acquire a fresh spirit for both of you when you come here. You will have plenty of room to indulge yourself in and a garden which will deserve your prose when you see it—flowers—trees and shady banks—ought we not to be happy and so indeed we are. . . . "

Mary had another reason to be happy that winter. She was once again pregnant. Although William and Allegra were adorable babies, Mary longed for a daughter of her own, particularly since she still mourned the tiny girl she had lost.

But finally even Mary's good news and the presence of loyal friends and companions did not soften Shelley's next blow. On March 27 the Lord Chancellor's edict called Shelley unfit to be the guardian of his children, citing among other evidence, his "atheistic" poem *Queen Mab*. The children were placed with a clergyman's family in Kent, and Shelley went into a decline.

All of Mary's sympathies were with her beloved husband as he worked through his misery. Her heart ached for him: "Sorrows and adversity had struck home," she wrote later.

> There are few who remember him sailing paper boats, and watching the navigation of his tiny craft with eagerness—or repeating with wild energy "The Ancient Mariner," and Southey's "Old Woman of Berkley"; but those who do will recollect that it was in such that he sheltered himself from the storms and disappointments, the pain and sorrow that beset his life.

While Shelley was at the lake trying to distract himself with his miniature ships—for the water was always soothing to his high-strung nerves—Mary would snatch a few hours to continue Frankenstein's saga. The book was taking form now. It was always a wrench to abandon her scientist and his Monster to return to the rest of her life. They had become as real to her as Shelley and the baby.

Finally, though, the day came when the book was completed. Mary entered a brief note in her diary: "May 14—Shelley reads 'History of the French Revolution' and corrects 'Frankenstein.' Write Preface. Finis."

It was both a relief and a loss to complete the book. Its writing had occupied nearly ten months. Mary had written valiantly day in and day out through one crisis after another: Fanny's death and Harriet's, the loss of Shelley and Harriet's children. She had taken only a day or two at a time away from her writing to make preparations for her own wedding and to assist Claire when baby Allegra was born. Sometimes she felt overwhelmed, frightened for the future. Her journal for January 24 records: "My William's birthday. How many changes have occurred during this little year; may the ensuing one be more peaceful, and my William's star be a fortunate one. . . ." But somehow she managed to keep her spirits even and discipline herself to continue the book that meant so much to her.

Now, with the manuscript neatly packed in a box and delivered to a publisher, Mary gave in to a nostalgic sadness. From her father's house in London where she had gone to await word from the publisher on *Frankenstein*'s acceptance, she wrote a wistful letter to Shelley at Marlow; she had been reading *Childe Harold*—the poem that Byron had written the third part of during the summer before at Geneva, while they had all been together. "It made me dreadfully melancholy," the letter says. "—The lake—the mountains and the faces associated with these scenes passed before me— Why is not life a continued moment where hours and days are not counted? . . ."

The summer, Mary knew, would be a waiting period. Back at Albion House in Marlow, she found the house full to the rafters: the vivacious Hunts and their five children, Claire and her baby, and of course Shelley, William, and faithful Elise, the nurse. Being a hostess, even when she was entertaining people she loved such as the Hunts, was a strain for Mary. For one thing, it was hard to set aside time for her own work. Still, she realized her home had to be open to all Shelley's friends, and of course there was her own strong sense of duty toward her family. This time, though, there were compensations; the Hunt children were adorable, and little Allegra was the prettiest and most spirited little girl Mary had ever seen. Playing with the children, Mary would daydream about the baby she was carrying.

The burden for all the household arrangements was squarely on Mary that summer. Shelley began his poem *The Revolt of Islam,* and was too engrossed in its creation to spend much time with anyone. What she needed, Mary decided, was a mind child of her own. With *Frankenstein* now beginning to go the rounds of the publishers—for John Murray had decided not to publish the terrifying story after all—Mary turned to the diary she and Shelley had kept just after they had eloped three years earlier. Together with Shelley, Mary whipped into shape for publication a series of lively little sketches about their travels through the continent. The little book, *A History of a Six Weeks' Tour*, was immediately accepted for publication by Thomas Hookham, who was a friend of Shelley's, and scheduled to appear in the bookstores during the fall of the year.

The late summer of 1817 brought another happy event. On September 2—just after her twentieth birthday—Mary went into speedy labor and delivered a little girl, whom she named Clara Everina. Mary was thrilled—the baby was healthy and alert, and best of all, she seemed to her mother to be the very image of Shelley! Blue-eyed and golden-haired like all of Mary's children, Clara seemed to duplicate in miniature her father's wide forehead, pointed chin, and cupid's-bow mouth.

With Clara's birth came a second piece of good news. Shelley succeeded in finding a publisher for *Frankenstein*—Messrs. Lackington, Allen and Co. Shelley himself wrote the preface for the first edition, which was to be announced as "a work of imagination," for issue early in 1818. Mary's Monster had found a home—now all there was to do was wait to see how it was received.

The fall of 1817 should have been, by all rights, a totally happy time for Mary. Two babies, two books—all this for a young woman just out of her teens. But the dark fate that stalked her throughout her life was at work again. Claire was in a "croaking humour" because of jealousy about Mary's writing. She knew that she had only vivacity and beauty, while Mary and Shelley had genius. "In this family," she once said sniffily, "if you haven't published a book, you're nothing." Besides Claire's sulks and moods, there were other problems around her. Byron was not taking much responsibility for baby Allegra, and it was increasingly clear that to avoid further gossip, the baby would somehow have to be placed under his care. Godwin was unrelenting in his cadging; debts, more debts, and the constant need to dodge creditors were haunting Shelley's life. Mary was learning to deal with these problems—she had a strong gallows humor and could make fun of her persecutors—but for Shelley these irritations were disastrous. His finely tuned nervous system revolted and, as always when his mind was under pressure, his body collapsed.

It wasn't only Mary who worried. Shelley's frail health alarmed his friends too. His indigestion and internal pains—and mostly those swift high fevers that would come and go—were a warning sign of the one of the most dread diseases of the century: tuberculosis. Shelley himself was frightened, so much so that he left Mary at home with three-week-old Clara to consult in London with an eminent doctor.

At Marlow Mary anxiously awaited for the diagnosis. She poured out her love and encouragement in a letter each night:

> Ah! my love, you cannot guess how wretched it was to see your languor and increasing illness. I now say to myself he is better—but then I watched you every moment and every moment was full of pain both to you and to me. Write my love, a long account of what Lawrence says—I shall be very anxious until I hear.

The answering letter did little to calm her fears. Dr. Lawrence did not exactly say it was tuberculosis—to say so would have been to seal Shelley's death warrant. But his recommendation all but made it clear: The Shelleys must leave damp Marlow at once for a better climate—either the sea air of the English coast or sunny Italy.

Mary favored England, but either choice would do as long as it saved Shelley. Mary's life had been stalked with death—her mother, Fanny, her first baby; and now if anything were to happen to Shelley, her very life would be over! Her letter left the choice to her husband:

> You tell me to decide between Italy and the sea— if your feelings are decided enough on the subject—if Italy would not give you far more pleasure than a settlement on the coast of Kent— If it would say so and so be it— Do you glow with the thoughts of a clear sky—pure air and burning sun— You would then enjoy life. For my own part I shall have tolerable health anywhere and for pleasure Italy certainly holds . . . a charming prospect.

"A charming prospect" was certainly what the Shelleys needed. Shelley in London awaiting diagnosis of his illness had no peace from other problems that Mary knew were eroding his frail health. "You are teased to death by all kinds of annoying affairs—dearest—how do I wish that I were with you," Mary wrote, and tried to cheer him up with a happy picture of herself at Marlow waiting for him, "surrounded by babes." But her thoughts were heavy, for it became clear that Shelley was once again in fear of imprisonment for debts and was trying, sick as he was, to raise money in London. All things considered, Italy was the place to go, Shelley decided, and loyal Mary, as usual, went along with his choice.

The house at Marlow was placed on the market and Mary began the tedious task of packing. Working between crates and barrels, Mary corrected the proofs for *A Six Weeks' Tour* and awaited news on the progress of *Frankenstein*, now being set in type. The long winter crawled slowly to a close: "January 3rd," reads Mary's journal, "Shelley unwell. Peacock passes the day here. Hogg comes in the evening." "January 4th. Shelley unwell. Talk with him."

Then, suddenly, everything fell into place. The house at Marlow was sold on January 25. On February 7 Shelley left for London, and Mary, staying behind to finish disposing of the house, followed on February 12. Three weeks in London for both, a chance to see some plays, go to the Opera. The first week of March saw *Frankenstein* in print at last. And now there was nothing further to keep them in England!

On board the ship to Calais, Shelley drowsed and Mary put a postscript on his unfinished letter to Leigh Hunt:

> Shelley is full of business, and desires me to finish this hasty note of our safety. The children are in high spirits, and very well. . . . We now depart for Italy, with very fine weather and good hopes.
>
> Farewell, my dear Friend, may you be happy.
>
> > Your affectionate friend,
> > Mary W.S.

8

"We Are Born to Love"

"We are born into the world to love, and there is something within us, which, from the instant that we live, more or less thirsts after its own likeness," Shelley wrote. No wonder it was no sacrifice for Mary to tailor her life according to Shelley's pattern. Shelley was not merely her lover, her husband, her companion, her teacher, her colleague. He was, quite simply, her other self.

It was remarkable how alike they were when their beginnings were so different. Mary was born into a family revered in radical, intellectual circles. Shelley's family was rich, titled, and conservative. His ancestors were country squires who husbanded the land, upheld the solid values of "county and church," rode to hounds, shot grouse and partridge, brought baskets of food to the poor at Christmas, and in general were the backbone of traditional, upper-class England.

Into this privileged world—an estate called Field Place, some forty miles from London, a place of glades, groves, birds, and butterflies—Percy Bysshe Shelley was born on August 4, 1792, to Timothy and Elizabeth Shelley. Bysshe (the name rhymes with fish), as his family called him, was the oldest of six surviving children. He had four sisters and a brother. The boy was beautiful, golden-haired, tall for his age, and slender. He seemed superbly equipped for the future his parents confidently took for granted: public and social life in which graceful oratory was the requirement to be a Sussex squire, politician, and landowner.

The boy was a rebel from the beginning. His father wrote about him, somewhat defensively, later in his life:

> I can assure you that I never gave him Liberties, that from six years of life he has never been kept one day from School when ought to be there, and in his Holydays I read the Classics and other Books with him in the full hopes of making him a good and gentlemanly Scholar.

The love of reading held—Shelley grew up to become one of the world's great readers, spending as much as sixteen hours a day with a book in hand—but every other aspect of his father's training went in one ear and out the other.

Young Shelley showed no interest in estate management. The overwhelming interests of his life—science and the supernatural as a way of penetrating the mysteries of the physical world, and what he later described in his preface to *Prometheus Unbound* as a "passion for reforming the world"—developed early in his life.

In the attic of Field Place was a closed room that Shelley and his sisters could enter through a trapdoor in the garret floor. Shelley made up stories about an "Alchemist, old and grey, with a long beard" who lived there. "Books and a lamp, with all the attributes of a picturesque fancy, were poured in our listening ears," wrote his sister Hellen. Alchemy, fiends, and spirits occupied the imagination of the boy and his audience: "We dressed ourselves in strange costumes . . . and Bysshe would take a fire-shovel and fill it with some inflammable liquid and carry it flaming into the kitchen and to the back door." Later, in his poem "Hymn to Intellectual Beauty," Shelley wrote:

While yet a boy I sought for ghosts, and sped
Through many a listening chamber, cave and ruin,
And starlight wood, with fearful steps pursuing
Hopes of high talk with the departed dead.

While the night was full of the voices of magic, the boy's days were spent listening to the pleas of those he saw oppressed by tyranny, poverty, and despotism. He rode through the Sussex lanes and roads with Lucas, his father's steward, meeting all too many people who were out of work. According to Lucas, "he would give lavishly and if he had no money with him, would borrow of me." At fourteen at a dance at Horsham, the elegantly dressed young lord was expected to lead forth a girl of rank and fashion; instead, he shocked his family and the other guests by choosing as his partner a young woman shyly sitting on the sidelines whom everyone knew had been seduced and "ruined" for society.

Syon House Academy, the school to which Shelley was sent at ten along with his cousin, Thomas Medwin, was hardly expected to cure the boy of these strange concerns. Sir Timothy put his confidence in Eton, the most prestigious prep school in England. The school's purpose, as its magazine *The Etonian* carefully explained, was "to polish the gems so as to reduce the separate parts to harmonize with the whole without destroying the individual beauty of each." Surely, when the "scholars" at Eton took Shelley under their wing, Sir Timothy reasoned, the boy's eccentricities would be "polished" into a wholesome individuality.

At fourteen, Shelley found himself in a whirlwind of boys. As "new boy"—and lacking any herd instinct—he saw himself as being apart from the whole school. Understanding him better than anyone else in the world, Mary based her character Derham, in her novel *Lodore* (published in 1835), on what he told her. Mary wrote:

> The boy was unlike the rest; he had wild fancies and strange inexplicable ideas. He said he was a mystery to himself—he was at once wise and foolish. The mere aspect of a grammar inspired him with horror, and a kind of delirious stupidity seized him in the classes; and yet he could discourse with eloquence, and pored with unceasing delight over books of the abstrusest philosophy. He seemed incapable of feeling the motives and impulses of other boys: when they jeered him he would answer gravely with some story of a

ghastly spectre, and tell wild legends of weird beings, who roamed through the dark fields by night, or sat wailing by the banks of streams: he was struck, he smiled and turned away; . . . he was the scoff, and butt, and victim of the whole school.

Perhaps Shelley was saved at Eton because there was nothing of the coward about him. He had too many resources of his own to be threatened by popular opinion. In time, without really trying, he managed to earn the respect of his classmates. He arrived at Eton with some training in the classics; he left with a mastery of them. Science continued to fascinate him; he had an "electric machine," designed after an invention of Benjamin Franklin's, with which he once electrified the doorknob of his room. He wrote verse, and finally a full-length Gothic romance titled *Zastrozzi*. The story was published, and even his father was impressed by his first paid literary work. He received forty pounds—a considerable sum in those days—and took eight Etonians out to an elegant dinner on part of this windfall.

While his budding literary career was being established, Shelley had more exciting things on his mind. One of his childhood companions was his cousin, Harriet Grove; and now, a young man of seventeen, he found himself in love with her. Harriet was fresh and pretty—and Shelley, as her brother wrote, "was at that time more attached than I can express."

But Shelley's imagination outstripped the possibilities. Harriet was a conventional girl. Shelley's "wild ideas" frightened her. "She became uneasy at the tone of his letters on speculative subjects," wrote her brother later, "at first consulting my mother, and subsequently my father also on the subject." The Groves were clearly unhappy at the idea of Shelley as a son-in-law, and Harriet, the dutiful daughter, turned him down.

Shelley went briefly into a decline. His sister Elizabeth watched him anxiously in his dejection. She insisted on accompanying him when he walked with his dog and gun. But for all his romantic imagination, Shelley was not one to die for love. He had been accepted at Oxford University, and he looked forward to throwing himself into his interests in science and literature.

Shelley's first friendship at Oxford was a lucky one. It was with Thomas Jefferson Hogg—a quiet boy with a whimsical sense of humor. Hogg was not interested in science, and he steered Shelley toward his own talents for ethics—moral questions about people's behavior toward each other. Shelley began to read Locke and Hume and, more important, on November 19 he ordered a copy of Godwin's *Political Justice.* The book instantly revived his interest in social and political questions. His early compassion for the poor and helpless became a concern for the masses, whom he saw as oppressed by a tyrannical political and economic system. He wrote a radical work which he called *St. Irvyne*, and a now-vanished essay called "An Essay on Love," during his first months at Oxford. Then, he and Hogg collaborated on a novel called *Leonora.* The publisher to whom he took it found it full of "dangerous opinions," and the young authors were forced to look for another printer.

The "dangerous opinions" that Shelley advanced

were his opposition to the British government, which he thought sacrificed the interests of the people to the welfare of the rich and titled, and organized religion. It was this last conviction that resulted in his expulsion from Oxford. Shelley and Hogg put together and had printed at their own expense a little pamphlet called *The Necessity of Atheism*. A hastily called tribunal of Oxford dons considered the tract and promptly closed the doors of the famous university to the young infidel.

Shelley's career at Oxford lasted only six months, but his usually conservative father was inclined to take the crisis in his stride. He decided Hogg was a bad influence and, to dislodge the friendship, he offered his son a voyage to the Greek Islands. Shelley refused. He also turned down Sir Timothy's alternative two plans: Shelley was to return to Field Place and be put under the "care and society" of a gentleman appointed by his father, and to run for Parliament under the sponsorship of the aristocratic Duke of Norfolk. His cousin, Charles Grove, wrote: "I recollect the indignation Bysshe expressed after that dinner at what he considered an effort made to shackle his mind, and introduce him into life as a mere follower of the Duke. His father was puzzled what to do when that plan failed."

Indeed, there was not much his father could do. Shelley had other interests to pursue. He met Leigh Hunt and established the groundwork for the friendship that would flower several years later. Hunt was then the editor of *The Examiner*, an intellectual magazine, and was already known as a writer, a painter, a scholar of the classics, fine arts, theater, music, and law—and, more important to Shelley, a radical thinker and atheist. Most engrossing of all, Shelley met a schoolmate of his sister's named Harriet Westbrook and, as swiftly as he did everything, he fell in love!

Harriet Westbrook was sixteen to Shelley's nineteen, a beautiful and strictly reared girl. At first Harriet was afraid of "Mad Shelley." "You may conceive with what horror I first heard that Percy was an atheist . . ." she wrote in a letter. "I wondered how he could live a moment professing such principles, and solemnly declared that he should never shake mine." But Shelley wrote to her, visited her, poured out his ideas in a steady stream of excited rhetoric, and soon won her. Shelley's plan surfaced—he would rescue her from her conservative, smothering family with the idea of "moulding a really noble soul into all that can make its nobleness useful and lovely." He whisked her away in August 1811, and they eloped to Scotland to be married.

Shelley resumed his friendship with Hogg, who had gone with them to Edinburgh and returned with them to York. Hogg fell in love with young Mrs. Shelley. "It was . . . agreeable to look at her," Hogg wrote. "She was always pretty, always bright, always blooming. . . . The ladies said of her that she always looked as if she had just stepped out of a glass case; and so indeed she did." Other, less agreeable matters occupied Shelley; he had fallen out with Sir Timothy, was having money problems, and again had become restless for adventure and purpose.

It was not long before he found his next cause: Irish independence. In that year, 1811, there was great uneasiness in Ireland because England was withholding civil rights from the people. Shelley's plan was to prepare the Irish to revolt. But his trip to Ireland—and a brief expedition to Wales as part of a Utopian group—proved to him that he was better as a poet than as a revolutionary. His radical action in Ireland consisted of no more than dropping little pamphlets he had written from his hotel room balcony, thrusting them into women's hoods, and some even more magical ways of propagandizing, such as sending his little booklets aloft in balloons and out to sea in glass bottles. His experiment in revolution ended, he returned to England to his life's work: outlining in his poems his ideal of the perfect world.

Shelley wrote the first of his great poems, *Queen Mab*, that year. The plot of the poem is simple: Queen Mab, a fairy, appears before a beautiful girl named Ianthe. She takes the blue-eyed, golden-haired young woman to her own palace in outer space. The two travel through the universe in Mab's celestial chariot until the earth, far behind, is only "the smallest light that twinkles in heaven." Finally they arrive at the fairy's palace, the Hall of Spells. There they take their places at an overhanging battlement, to better view the universe and conceive of time itself.

This framework gives Shelley a chance to explain his three-fold vision. Queen Mab tells the girl about the Past, where the glory of the world passes away because of "wealth, that curse of Man"; the Present, with its evils of tyranny, poverty, injustice, and misery; and the Future, in which the world is redeemed by faith in the "Spirit of Nature: all-sufficing power." The poem reflects Godwin's ideas—an assault against

Church and government, formalized education, custom and convention. It also has some ideas that were strictly Shelley's—and that he would share with Mary—such as vegetarianism. But the poem also contains hints of the direction that Shelley's more mature work would take: the Platonic belief that a kindly World Spirit permeates life while "happiness and science dawn though late upon the earth."

Queen Mab was dedicated to Harriet, but by the time it was published, Shelley no longer was in love with his wife. He had met Mary and found his ideal of love. In Godwin's circle, the young poet had everything he sought: a teacher and mentor in the old philosopher, and in his daughter a mate of whom he felt (as he wrote to his friend Hogg) "so intimately are our natures now united, that I feel whilst I describe her excellencies as if I were an egoist expatiating upon his own perfections."

From the earliest days of their courtship, Shelley's love for Mary was an exchange of sensitivity, creativity, scholarship. He would read his poetry aloud to her under the willows at Mary Wollstonecraft's grave, while Claire, taken along as a decoy, made herself scarce in the nearby meadow. He taught her Greek; she read aloud to him from Voltaire, Locke, Hume. Their jointly kept diary records at the end of every year a list of books they read: Mary's list for 1815 includes Byron's *Lara*, Milton's *Paradise Lost*, Shakespeare's plays, and several books by her father and her mother. Shelley's list is heavily Greek and Latin: Seneca's tragedies, works by Herodotus, Homer, Thucydides.

Throughout their life together, Mary's and Shelley's work represented phases of each other's thinking. *Frankenstein* is subtitled *The Modern Prometheus.* The Prometheus theme—the ancient Greco-Roman myth in which Prometheus stole fire from heaven for the benefit of mankind, thus symbolically creating life—was a vital part of Shelley's creative body of work. It was a shared theme: "A certain similarity all the best writers of any particular age are marked with, from the spirit of that age working upon all," Shelley wrote later in a letter to his publishers Charles and James Ollier, thus acknowledging not only the interplay of his thinking with Mary's, but also the influence of Goethe's poem *Prometheus* and Beethoven's *Promethean Ballet*, performed at Vienna in 1801.

The Promethean archetype emerged in Mary's work as the scientist and his Monster, and in Byron's poem "Prometheus," dated Diodati, July 1816—the summer that Mary wrote *Frankenstein*. The cross-pollination of creative ideas also shows up in Byron's poem *Manfred*, written shortly afterward. Like Dr. Frankenstein, Byron's protagonist draws from "Withered bones, and skulls, and heap'd up dust" in "caves of death conclusions most forbidden."

The parallels in Shelley's and Mary's work are strongest in Shelley's drama *The Cenci*, completed in May 1819, and an unpublished novella by Mary entitled *Mathilda*, which she wrote that same summer. Shelley, in fact, had originally suggested that Mary write the story he used—a tale of a father's unnatural love for his daughter, and his murder at her hands.

But more than by the parallels in their work, Mary and Shelley's creative life together was marked by the mutual encouragement they gave to each other. It was through Mary's undemanding love that Shelley matured as a poet, growing from the idealistic young reformer who had pursued liberty and justice in England, Wales, and Ireland to the fully developed man of letters who used allegory as the vehicle for his developing social and religious ideas.

The first of his great poems, *Alastor*, written the year after his elopement with Mary, is autobiographical. It expresses his despair over the exhaustion of his revolutionary ideals and aspirations. The second, "Hymn to Intellectual Beauty," written after the summer he and Mary spent in Switzerland, realizes a truth he had not understood in *Alastor*: ideal beauty, which "gives grace and truth to life's unquiet dream," cannot be fully incorporated in earthly form or clasped in human shape. *The Revolt of Islam*, written just before he left England for the last time, a poem which begins with a beautiful dedication to Mary, shows the revival of Shelley's hopes for humanity. But it was not until they reached Italy that he found complete fulfillment of his vision.

Shelley's first Italian opus was the first act of *Prometheus Unbound*. The poem took him nearly a year and a half to write, for it was interrupted by excursions into other work, and by the events of his life. Its subject is what was wrong with the world in Shelley's time, what sort of miracle was needed to redeem humanity, and what the world would be like if the miracle took place—as Shelley believed it would. His conviction that he and his contemporary writers were "the companions and forerunners of some unimagined change in our social condition or the opinions which cement it" was expressed in prose, in his "A

Philosophical View of Reform" of 1820, and in "A Defense of Poetry," written in 1821. It appears in lyrical poetry in "Ode to the West Wind"—his prayer that his ideas for humanity would be driven over the universe, quickening a new birth of thought and action as the wind quickens the leaves. And it appears, in final form, in "The Triumph of Life," a poem he was never to finish.

Indeed, Italy so marked Shelley's golden age as a poet that after the first few weeks of ill health, he seemed nearly impervious to the problems around him and the tragedies that were in store.

The first of the problems was, as always, Claire. Byron was in Venice—close enough, but somehow out of reach. He refused to answer Claire's letters asking for help with baby Allegra's upbringing and support. Shelley's soft heart was touched. He immediately wrote a tactful but forthright letter which Byron *had* to answer. Byron's terms were harsh: He would take Allegra if Claire would give up her claim to the little girl. Allegra was to be brought up a Catholic, he wrote, and an Italian. As an illegitimate child she had no future in English society—she must be separated from her British mother and prepared eventually to make a decent marriage with a well-born Italian. Claire, selfish in everything except her genuine love for her baby, reluctantly agreed, and a month after they had arrived in Italy, Mary, Shelley, and Claire bade tearful good-byes to the baby as she set off with Elise, the nurse, to Venice and her father.

An unpleasant task now chalked off, Shelley and Mary turned to happier matters. They still had no permanent residence in Italy—a trip to Lake Como in search for a house had not turned up anything they liked. Now their travels took them to Leghorn (Livorno), in the north of Italy. There, a wonderful treat awaited them. Maria Gisborne—formerly Mrs. Reveley, the neighbor to whom Mary's father had proposed marriage soon after Mary Wollstonecraft's death—renewed her friendship with Mary. The Shelleys were delighted to have found her. "A long conversation about my mother and father," Mary wrote happily in her diary.

The early part of the summer found the Shelleys somewhat settled. Shelley rented a house at the Bagni di Lucca. He installed his family and Claire and turned his attention toward his new project—a translation of Plato's *Symposium* from the ancient Greek, which he managed to complete in ten days. Mary, too, was occupied. The first reviews of *Frankenstein* had come in. It was exciting to read them: The critics were frightened, repelled, and awed, but none of them missed the power of the book!

Only Claire was still miserable, achingly lonely for her baby. Byron had placed Allegra with Mrs. Richard Belgrave Hoppner, the wife of the British Consul-General in Venice. Only he could help her, she told Shelley. If only he would go to see Byron and plead her case, if only she could see the little girl! Shelley had no choice; he and Claire packed up and set off for Venice to confront Byron.

Byron, an ogre in his letters to Claire, was mild and reasonable with Shelley. Certainly, he agreed, it would be all right for Allegra to spend a week with her mother. To reassure Shelley that he meant only the best by his daughter, he took him to meet Mrs.

Hoppner. Shelley promptly wrote a letter to Mary. The baby was in good hands; he liked Mrs. Hoppner—she had "hazel eyes and sweet looks—rather Maryish." Besides, the trip had yielded a dividend: Byron had offered the Shelleys the use of his estate. Mary, he instructed, was to pack up the children and herself and meet him.

Mary's trip, begun with excitement and high hopes, ended with the death of her second daughter. Clara had been feverish and cranky when Mary set out; after four days of hot, dusty travel in a stagecoach, the little girl was dangerously ill. Shelley made a frenzied search for a doctor, but Clara was beyond saving. Mary attempted to take the tragedy in her stride. Only Shelley saw through her stoic calm. He told Claire that this "unexpected stroke reduced Mary to a kind of despair."

Trouble and misery always made Shelley productive. Back at Este with Allegra and Claire—Mary and Shelley had convinced Byron to let Claire have her baby for two weeks—he wrote "Julian and Maddalo," a poem about himself and Byron. Mary played with William during the day, and in the evening she wrote long letters to her father. Godwin, though, was less comfort than ever. His letter to her telling her, "We seldom indulge long in depression and mourning, except when we think secretly that there is something very refined in it," was the crowning touch. Shelley went into a rage at Godwin's callousness, and threatened to intercept his letters so that Mary would not be able to read them.

In November, Allegra was returned to the Hoppners and Mary and Shelley were free to leave Venice. They spent the winter traveling chiefly between Rome and Naples. But now Mary's sorrow had hardened into a cold, withdrawn depression. Try as he might, Shelley could not escape the contagion. He took time out from writing *Prometheus Unbound* to express his feelings about Mary:

> I am far happier than thou,
> Lady whose imperial brow
> Is endiademed with woe.

And in "Stanzas Written in Dejection, Near Naples," he writes about his own:

Alas! I have nor hope nor health,
Nor peace within nor calm around . . .
Nor fame, nor power, nor love, nor pleasure. . . .
I could lie down like a tired child,
And weep away the life of care
Which I have borne and still must bear. . . .

Throughout all this, though, Shelley continued to write. Italy itself was an inspiration, reinforcing his sense of the beauty of nature as part of the World Spirit for good—the serene, ordered universe he envisioned and, as a poet, saw as his calling to describe and exalt. In his beautiful prose, too, he described the landscape: "I walk forth in the purple and golden light of an Italian evening, and return by star or moonlight through this scene. The elms are just budding and the warm spring winds bring unknown odours, all sweet from the country. . . ." This oneness with his world allowed Shelley—even at his saddest—to work with some serenity; he completed the first act of *Prometheus Unbound* in Naples, and in April 1819 he had added two more acts.

But Italy, beautiful Italy, shortly turned on him. The warm climate, which he had hoped would rescue his ailing health, had claimed the life of his daughter from "Roman fever," and now threatened his son's. Mary, pregnant again, brought him the news that little William was suffering from "summer complaint"—the malady that could be dangerous to a small child in a hot climate.

William was by all odds the Shelleys' favorite child. Bright and full of fun, he chattered away in three languages, to his parents' utter delight. Besides, he was beautiful and the picture of health: "The silken fineness of his hair, the transparency of his complexion, the animation and deep blue color of his eyes were the astonishment of everyone," his father wrote of him.

William's sudden illness mobilized Shelley into action. He sent for Dr. Bell, the best physician in the area. Shelley stayed at the boy's bedside—passing sixty hours without sleep—but the little boy rallied, slipped, and then passed away on June 7. He was buried in the Protestant cemetery in Rome.

Neither Shelley nor Mary could any longer bear to be reminded of the scenes associated with the dead child. They fled to Leghorn to be near the comforting Gisbornes. Mary was inconsolable. She sat rigidly day after day, too grief-stricken even to speak. For the first time, Shelley could not reach her; sometimes she didn't answer him when he spoke to her. Heartbroken, Shelley wrote:

My dearest Mary, wherefore hast thou gone,
And left me in this dreary world alone?
Thy form is here indeed—a lovely one—
But thou art fled, gone down a dreary road. . . .

Writing *The Cenci*—that story of murder, lust, vengeance—distracted Shelley from his mourning for his baby and from his loneliness for his wife. But Mary's depression was so deep she did not even want to work. Instead, she took some art lessons with Amelia Curran, whom she had known in England. Then, finally, after "five wretched months without a child," she gave birth to a son, Percy Florence. The spell of misery was broken.

Italy, the paradise Shelley had sought, was beginning to pall, and in the midst of all his sorrow, nostalgically he turned his eyes back to England. At the end of the summer of 1819 he had written to Peacock:

I most devoutly wish I were living near London. . . . What are mountains, trees, heaths or even the glorious and ever-beautiful sky . . . to friends? Social enjoyment, in some form or other, is the alpha and omega of existence. All that I see in Italy . . . is nothing; it dwindles in the mind, when I think of some familiar forms of scenery, little perhaps in themselves, over which old remembrances have thrown a delightful colour. How we prize what we despise when present. So the ghosts of our dead associations rise and haunt us, in revenge for our having let them starve, and abandoned them to perish.

Actually two events turned his eyes back to his native country. England was in the throes of what nearly turned into a civil war. In the north of England workingmen in the burgeoning new factories revolted against the owners. A meeting of reformists in Manchester on August 16 had been pronounced illegal, and to disperse the crowd, a cavalry charge was made and several laborers were killed or wounded. Shelley's furies once again surfaced. He wrote three poemsin anguished protest: *Mask of Anarchy*, "Sonnet: England in 1819," and "Song to the Men of England," with an impassioned admonition to the workers:

> Sow seed—but let no tyrant reap;
> Find wealth—let no imposter heap;
> Weave robes—let not the idle wear;
> Forge arms—in your defence to bear.

The second event that recalled Shelley's memories and thoughts back to his birthplace was the untimely death of John Keats. Shelley felt that it was the reviewers who had hastened the young poet's end. He saw Keats—as he saw himself—a victim of oppression, the romantic symbol of the poet hounded by the world's brutality. He knew that he, himself, "in another's fate now wept his own."

But in the end it was not England, but Italy, that betrayed Shelley's dream of happiness. The last tragedy of his short life—the death of four-year old Allegra—like the loss of his own two children, was, once again, a result of an epidemic disease that flourished in the humid, sticky Italian summer.

Shelley's feeling for Allegra was as strong as though she had been his own child. It was partly because he was fond of her caustic, wild, vivacious mother, partly too because of his love for Byron, but mostly because little Allegra herself was such an enchantress. A pretty child, as her father described her in a letter, "remarkably intelligent and a great favourite with everybody . . . she has very blue eyes . . . fair curly hair, and a devil of spirit," Allegra had both Mary and Shelley wrapped around her little finger. Then, too, there was Shelley's overactive conscience at work. He and Mary were responsible for the little girl's death, he thought. In the spring of 1821 when Claire, then working as a governess in Florence, had learned that Byron had placed the baby in a convent in Bagnacavallo, she had protested that the poor sanitation and intense heat were dangerous to the baby's health. Shelley and Mary sought to reassure her—in fact Mary wrote a calming letter: "Your great anxiety for Allegra's health is unfounded. . . . Venice, its stinking canals and dirty streets is enough to kill any child . . . but the town of Romagna . . . enjoys the best air in Italy." Alas, Claire was right; Allegra died of typhus, a plague that swept through the town.

There was to be no more great poetry. "Poetry is the best and happiest moment of the best and happiest minds," Shelley had written in his essay "A Defence of Poetry." Now his fragile nervous system was in jeopardy. Soothing music, quiet beauty, and, as always, the sea and boats were what he needed, were all his nerves would handle. Sometime earlier, a boyhood chum named Edward Williams had appeared again in his life. Williams was living with a beautiful young woman who had taken his name, although they were not legally married. Jane Williams had the gift of quieting Shelley's troubled soul with her beauty and serenity. Shelley delighted in her music; he bought her a guitar and they would spend afternoons together while she played and sang in her gentle, hypnotic voice.

But mostly it was the sea that calmed him. On May Day, 1822, the Shelleys and Williamses took possession of the Casa Magni in the fishing village of San Terenzo. Byron's friend Edward Trelawney, who became a frequent visitor to the house, described it as more like a boathouse or a bathing house than a place to live. Its ground floor was used for storing produce and tackle; the veranda was actually built over the Gulf of Spezia, and at high tide the waves washed against the walls.

Despite its romantic surroundings, the house was gloomy—all the more so because Claire had returned to the Shelleys and the atmosphere was heavy with her mourning. Mary, too, was melancholy; she was once again pregnant, and feeling tired and ill. Shelley, his eyes fixed on the horizon, waited eagerly for the delivery of a boat he was having built for him in Genoa. At last the boat arrived, and without delay Shelley and Williams took her out for a trial run. "Williams declares her to be perfect," Shelley wrote in a letter, "and I participate in his enthusiasm. . . . [S]he passes the small boats as a comet might pass the dullest planet of heaven."

Shelley was thoroughly distracted by his new plaything. The little boat that he called the *Ariel* was the first truly seaworthy craft he had ever owned, and after several short sails in the bay, he pronounced it ready for a real voyage. At the end of June his old friends the Hunts arrived in Genoa to visit Byron and Trelawney. There was now a perfect reason for him to sail off toward the distant horizon. He would meet Leigh and Marianne Hunt in Leghorn and bring them back for a visit. Mary had misgivings. She hated the house, and could not face the trial of having the large Hunt family thrust upon her. But Shelley prevailed. He would not be gone long, he told her. And when he came back there would be time for the two of them to escape on the boat and read to each other in drowsy laziness on the blue waters of La Spezia.

On July 1, 1822, Shelley, Edward Williams, and a young sailor named Charles Vivian set sail. Mary watched from the terrace. Two or three times she called him back and then, at last, she returned to her bed and cried bitterly. It was to be their last parting.

9

The Heart Snatched from the Fire

The weeks before Shelley set out for the last time on his little boat were as strange and terrible as anything in *Frankenstein*.

First there was Mary's brush with death. On June 16 she had a miscarriage. "I was so ill that for seven hours I lay nearly lifeless," she wrote later to Mrs. Gisborne, "kept from fainting by brandy, vinegar eau de cologne &c. . . . They all thought and so did I at one time that I was about to die. . . ." Over the objections of Claire and Jane, who wanted to wait for the doctor, Shelley sent for ice and packed it around Mary's body. It stopped her hemorrhage and saved her life.

Then, no sooner was Mary unsteadily on her feet again than there was another visitation of horror: the eerie forecast of Shelley's death.

Mary was awakened from a sound sleep by Shelley's

screams. Panic-stricken, she jumped out of bed to get Jane Williams. By the time she returned Shelley was sitting up in bed, white and shaken.

"I had a dream," he told them tremulously. "I saw Edward and Jane. Their bodies were lacerated, their bones were starting through their skin, their faces were pale—yet stained with blood. Then Edward spoke: 'Get up Shelley the sea is flooding the house & it is all coming down.' "

"In my dream, I got up," Shelley went on. "I went to the window that looked out at the terrace and the sea, and I saw the sea rushing in. Suddenly my vision changed, and I saw myself strangling Mary!"

Mary and Jane managed to quiet him, and after a day or two the incident was more or less forgotten. But what was even more frightening to Mary was that Jane, too, had had a vision. While Shelley was given to hallucinations and nervous attacks, Jane was a sensible, level-headed woman, and when Jane reported fearfully that she had been standing on the terrace when she thought she saw Shelley pass by the window and then suddenly disappear, a hideous foreboding overtook Mary. Surely, she thought in her troubled heart, there was another tragedy not far off.

The worry was not quieted until several days after Shelley set off on the *Ariel*. A note from him arrived. The Hunts would not be coming back with him, he wrote, for Marianne was not feeling well. The letter, though, was cheerful and reassuring. "How are you my best Mary?" it asked, and went on to inquire whether she was "not more reconciled to staying at Lerici [Casa Magni] at least during the summer." Mary folded the note, put it in a drawer, and sat back calmly to wait for Shelley's return.

July 8—the day that Shelley was expected back—dawned, a day so stormy that Mary and Jane decided that Shelley had sensibly postponed sailing. But the next two days were calm, and Mary and Jane waited expectantly. Then on July 12 there was another letter; this one from Hunt, addressed to Shelley. The weather was so bad on Monday when Shelley sailed, Hunt wrote, that he was concerned about Shelley's return. How did the trip go? he asked.

In mounting terror Mary, still weak from her illness, and Jane hired a carriage and sped to Leghorn. There they heard no answers, only more questions. Hunt had seen them set forth—he knew nothing beyond that. Neither did Trelawney or Byron. As best he could, Trelawney tried to calm the women's fears. Surely Shelley had landed on some other shore, he told them. Mary and Jane, anxious to believe him, allowed him to accompany them home by carriage to await further news.

All hope ended on July 19. Trelawney had indeed found Shelley and Williams. Their bodies had washed up on the shore. In Shelley's pocket there was a slim volume with the pages turned back. It was Keats' *Endymion*—the poem he had been reading when his ship overturned.

Italian law required that the bodies be cremated in order to prevent the spread of disease. A sorrowful little party met on the beach to watch Shelley's funeral pyre prepared. Shelley's waterwashed body burned slowly. Suddenly, at the last moment, Trelawney reached into the fire and brought out Shelley's heart. The heart, miraculously uncharred, he gave to Mary.

It was Mary's own valiant heart that stood her in good stead for the rest of her life—the years that she would stand alone, a woman without protection in a society that relegated widows to poverty and obscurity.

The courage for her new life came slowly. For nearly three months she moved mechanically, in a fog. She got up in the morning to numbing sorrow, took care of little Percy Florence, went into her lonely bed at night too full of sadness even to weep. And then, the diary resumes:

"October 2. On the 8th of July I finished my journal. This is a curious coincidence. The date still remains—the fatal 8th—a monument to show that all ended then. Am I to begin again?"

To begin again—but how? Mary's diary continues heartbrokenly:

First, I have no friend. For eight years I communicated with unlimited freedom, with one whose genius, far transcending mine, awakened and guided my thoughts. I conversed with him . . . obtained new lights from him; and my mind was satisfied. Now I am alone—oh how alone! The stars may behold my tears, and the winds drink my sighs. . . . No eye answers mine. . . . What a change! O, my beloved Shelley! how often during these happy days—happy though checquered—I thought how superiorly gifted I had been in being united to one to whom I could unveil myself, and who could understand me! Well, then, now I am reduced to these white pages, which I am to blot with dark imagery. As

I write, let me think what he would have said if, speaking thus to him, he could have answered me.

There, alone in her room, Mary made her decision. From now on, she would write into her diary as though she were speaking to Shelley. The dialogue begins immediately. "As I write, let me think what he would have said . . . if he could have answered me. . . . 'Seek to know your own heart and, learning what it best loves, try to enjoy that.' "

Looking deep into her own heart, Mary came out with her course of action:

> Well, I cast my eyes around, and look forward to the bounded prospect in view. . . . Those I most loved are gone forever. . . . Literary labours, the improvement of my mind, and the enlargement of my ideas, are the only occupations that elevate me from my lethargy. Father, mother, friend, husband, children . . . all except you, my poor boy [Percy Florence] (and you are necessary to the continuance of my life), all are gone and I am left to fulfil my task. So be it.

And so it was. For the rest of her life, Mary knew that her task was to continue her writing and to take care of her son. Percy Florence was "the only chain that links me to time," she wrote, her only reason for living: "But for you, I should be free." "Freedom," sadly, meant quitting this life: "You are free, my Shelley," she wrote a few days later, "while I, your poor chosen one, am left to live as I may."

But how to do it? First, Mary was strapped financially; with Shelley gone, she had no funds other than the few pounds she had on hand. Jane Williams had left to join friends in England, and Claire, always Mary's responsibility somehow, had to be shipped off to Vienna to her brother. Mary turned for assistance to Byron. The poet, generous as always in his intentions toward her, offered to negotiate with Sir Timothy about Mary and her son.

Byron's good intentions came to nothing. Sir Timothy never forgave either his dead son nor Mary for the "disgrace" they had brought upon him. Sir Timothy would provide for Percy as his grandson—send him to Harrow and even to Oxford, if Mary would hand the little boy over to him or to a guardian he appointed, instead of raising him herself!

Mary's answer was swift and sure. *Never!* Percy would be hers and his father's through her! Mary was willing to abide any condition to get her son's rightful inheritance for him, but *never* at the cost of cutting Percy off from herself or from the memory of his own father.

Regretfully, Mary thanked Byron for all he had tried to do for her. Spending time with "Albe" was extremely painful. For all his goodness to her, he intensified her loneliness. Listening to his voice, she remembered the nightly sessions at Diodati when she, a pale, shy eighteen-year-old, would sit quietly in a corner thrilling to the conversation between Shelley and Byron. Now, she wrote in her diary, when "Albe speaks and Shelley does not answer, it is as thunder without rain . . . and I listen with an unspeakable melancholy. . . . Albe, his mere presence and voice, has the power of exciting . . . deep and shifting emotions within me."

All in all, it was time to leave Italy—beautiful Italy where she and Shelley had gone with such high hopes years earlier, and where she had lost so many of those she loved: Clara, William, Allegra, and Shelley himself. Time to return with Percy to England, to her own family and "the only act of pleasure that remains," to collect Shelley's poetry, published and unpublished, and write his biography as an "invaluable treasure" for her son.

Leaving Italy was bittersweet. She delayed it for nearly a year. Finally, she felt she had no further reason to stay. The Hunts, with whom she had lived after Shelley's death, were poor, her own chances of settling with Sir Timothy for an allowance for Percy were hampered by distance, and finally there was an open break with Byron over money that he owed Shelley for a bet. " 'Glad of a quarrel, straight I clap the door,' " Mary wrote to Jane Williams, and prepared for the long journey across the Alps to France, and then by ship to England.

During the year she had spent in Italy, in what she called "the gulph of melancholy," Mary had lost track of her "hideous progeny"—*Frankenstein*. But a surprise awaited her on her return. Godwin took her to the theater. Mary wrote a letter to Leigh Hunt the next day:

But lo and behold! I found myself famous—Frankenstein had prodigious success as a drama and was about to be repeated for the 23rd night at the English Opera House. The play bill amused me extremely, for in the list of dramatis personae came The Monster by Mr. T. Cooke; Wallack looked very well as F[rankenstein]. . . . The stage represents a room with a staircase leading to F.'s workshop—he goes to it and you see his light in a small window, through which a frightened servant peeps, who runs off in terror when F. exclaims 'It lives'!—Presently F. himself rushes in horror and trepidation from the room and while still expressing his agony and terror, the Monster throws down the door of the laboratory, leaps the staircase and presents his unearthly and monstrous person on the stage. The story is not well managed—but Cooke played the Monster's part extremely well—his seeking as it were for support—his trying to grasp at the sounds he heard—all he does indeed was well managed and executed. I was much amused and it appeared to excite a breathless eagerness in the audience. They continue to play it even now.

Mary realized some profits from the stage production and even more from a new edition of *Frankenstein* that her father had arranged for in her absence. Money, though, was still the problem. Mary wrote to Lady Shelley; her tact in appealing to her son's grandmother resulted in a meeting with Sir Timothy's lawyers, and she received a small sum—one hundred pounds and a plea for patience. The sum was enough to enable her to leave Godwin's house and set up her own place: "My lodgings are neat and quiet," she wrote to the Hunts, "my servant good—my boy in delightful health and very happy and amiable."

Dealing with Sir Timothy about Shelley's work, though, was far more difficult. Mary was determined to bring Shelley's poetry out in a collected edition. Her love played a part in her lifelong dedication to editing Shelley's manuscripts, but there was more to it than that. Mary had in addition to her own genius as a writer a highly developed critical sense. Even if Shelley had been a mere acquaintance, she would have recognized his poetry for what it was, and her strong sense of justice, part of her legacy from Godwin and Mary Wollstonecraft, would have smarted at the idea that Shelley's work was to be lost to the world because he had had the bad luck to have a narrow-minded, bigoted father!

One way or another, Mary resolved to get around the crusty old man, and when a friend of Hunt's, Bryan Waller Procter, offered to guarantee the expense of an edition of Shelley's poetry, Mary asked Hunt to write a biographical introduction, while her behind-the-scenes editing would be anonymous. The poems were published in 1824 and sold well, but Mary's scheme failed. Sir Timothy threatened to stop the small allowance he was making Mary on behalf of Percy Florence if any biography or edition of the Shelley work was published while he was alive.

Meanwhile, Mary struggled with her own writing. Her novel *Valperga* was published just before she returned to England, but she was having heavy trouble with the new one, *The Last Man.* Her dark mood, loneliness, and mourning again overtook her and she could not write. Night after night she found herself sleepless, her only refuge her diary. "My imagination is dead, my genius lost, my energies sleep," she wrote. "Amidst all the depressing circumstances that weigh on me, none sinks deeper than the failure of my intellectual powers; nothing I write pleases me."

In this pit of despair Mary received shocking news. Byron had gone on his last adventure: Fighting at the front at Missolonghi in the cause of Greek independence, he had been stricken with malaria and died.

Mary forgot her grievances against the dashing poet in the flood of memories his death brought. "I knew him in the bright days of youth," she wrote in her journal.

> When neither care nor fear had visited me—before death had made me feel my mortality, and the earth was the scene of my hopes. Can I forget our evening visits to Diodati? Our excursions on the lake, when he sang the Tyrolese Hymn and his voice harmonized with winds and waves? Can I forget his attentions and consolations to me during my deepest misery? Never.
>
> Albe—the dear capricious, fascinating Albe—has left this desert world. . . .

But oddly enough, the shock of Byron's death galvanized Mary into going back to work. "I feel my powers again," she wrote a few weeks later, "and this is, of itself, happiness; the eclipse of winter is passing from my mind. I shall again feel the enthusiastic glow of composition; again, as I pour forth my soul on paper, feel the winged ideas arise, and enjoy the delight of expressing them. . . ."

The Last Man is indeed a pouring forth of Mary's soul. It is, like *Frankenstein,* a novel that points to the future, and like *Frankenstein* it is peopled with characters based on those dearest to her: Shelley, Godwin, even Byron. While it does not use the form of science fiction as *Frankenstein* does, it deals with political theory and advanced ideas about government that were scarcely foreseen in Mary's day. The book's setting is the twenty-first century. England is no longer a monarchy in the novel, but rather a republic. By some odd coincidence, Mary named the fictional ousted British ruling family Windsor—the surname of the present monarchs, who did not succeed to the throne until 1917!

In the main character, ". . . the sensitive and excellent Adrian, loving all, and beloved by all . . ." Mary recreated Shelley as she knew him.

> He often left us, and wandered by himself in the woods, or sailed his little skiff, his books his only companions. He was often the gayest of our party, at the same time that he was . . . visited by fits of despondency; his slender frame seemed over-charged with the weight of life, and his soul appeared rather to inhabit his body than unite with it.

Like Shelley, Adrian was considered mad by those who had no sympathy for his liberal ideas. His plans for diminishing the power of the aristocracy and equalizing wealth and privilege through thought, rather than direct political action, were Shelley's, derived from Godwin and brought to maturity through his identification with "the Greek sages."

The plot of *The Last Man* centers around a plague that wipes out civilization, leaving one man alive. It was a theme that Mary knew well! "The last man!" she wrote in her journal in May of 1824. "Yes, I can well describe that solitary being's feelings, feeling myself as the last relic of a beloved race, my companions extinct before me."

For several years the only hedge Mary had against loneliness was Jane Williams. Her son was still too young to be a companion, her father too full of his own problems. The shared tragedy of their both losing their husbands on Shelley's ill-fated little boat made Mary feel very close to Jane. Surely in all the world, Jane was most likely to understand her sorrow and loneliness. But even while she was writing: "I love Jane better than any other human being," she had the nagging knowledge that Jane "but slightly returns this affection." In fact, although she was deeply hurt after spending a month's vacation with Jane the following August to overhear Jane say: "Thank God it is over," she was unprepared for Jane's final, terrible treachery. Jane, who had been flattered by the attention that Shelley had paid to her in Italy, had gone around telling people that Shelley was secretly in love with *her*!

Mary was shattered by Jane's betrayal. It was all the harder to take because Mary knew *she* had been such a good friend to Jane. Shelley's boyhood friend, Hogg, had fallen in love with Jane, and although Hogg had been cold and unfriendly toward Mary since Shelley's death, Mary swallowed her disappointment and encouraged Jane to "marry" Hogg. It wasn't important whether Hogg was kind to *her*, Mary thought; what mattered was *Jane's* happiness. Now Mary's hurt was so deep that she had trouble even writing about it:

Journal, 13th July—My friend has proved false and treacherous! Miserable discovery. For four years I was devoted to her, and I earned only ingratitude. Not for worlds would I attempt to transfer the deathly blackness of my meditations to these pages. Let no trace remain save the deep bleeding hidden wounds of my lost heart of such a tale of horror and despair. Writing, study, quiet, such remedies I must seek. . . .

Jane was upset over Mary's reaction, for Mary had what amounted to a nervous breakdown. She had meant no harm, Jane wept to Mary, and in truth, she had no idea that her cattiness would cut so deep. But Mary could not forgive her: "If I revert to my devotion to you," she wrote

it is to prove that no worldly motives could estrange me from the partner of my miseries—the sweet girl whose beauty, grace and gentleness were to me so long the sole charms of my life. . . . Could any but yourself have destroyed such engrossing and passionate love? And what are the consequences of the change? When I first heard that you did not love me—every hope of my life deserted me—the depression I sunk under, and to which I now am prey, undermines my health— How many hours this dreary winter I have paced my solitary room driven nearly to madness. . . .

But if Mary was victimized in her friendship with Jane, she was the one who had the upper hand in her romances with men.

Mary had returned to England a twenty-five-year-old widow. She had always been a pretty girl; now she was a beauty. "Her well shaped, golden head, almost always a little bent and drooping," wrote Mary Cowden Clarke, the daughter of one of Godwin's friends, describing her,

> Her marble white shoulders and arms statuesquely visible in the perfectly plain black velvet gown which the custom of that time allowed to be cut low, and which her own taste adopted; her thoughtful, earnest eyes; the short upper lip and intellectually curved mouth, with a certain close compressed and decisive expression while she listened and a relaxation into fuller redness and mobility when speaking; her exquisitely formed, white, dimpled, small hands, with rosy palms, and plumply commencing fingers, that tapered into tips as slender and delicate as those of a Vandyke portrait.

This combination of delicate beauty—and the defenselessness of widowhood—made Mary nearly irresistible to men, as she suddenly discovered.

The first man to fall in love with the young widow was a handsome American actor, playwright, and songwriter (still remembered for his song "Home, Sweet Home") named John Howard Payne. Mary was twenty-seven at the time, Payne six years older and one year older than Shelley would have been if he had lived. Payne was a friend of several people important in the literary world whom Mary already knew—Sir Walter Scott and John Murray, the publisher, among others. Mary met Payne—and his good friend, Washington Irving, the American author of "The Legend of Sleepy Hollow"—at the same time, at a party in Paris on her way home from Italy.

The friendship with Payne was pleasant enough for Mary. She loved the theater and Payne had an endless supply of tickets to all the new shows. Then, too, Payne had access to social circles that Mary felt were not open to her because of her "scandalous" early relationship with Shelley, and because she had been close to that controversial figure, Byron. In the early days of her love affair and marriage to Shelley, being alone with him was enough for Mary; but now she sought "society." It was pleasant being welcomed to salons and dinner parties escorted by Payne. Unfortunately, sharing good times was not enough for *him.* Payne fell madly in love.

To keep the friendship light enough required a balancing act. Mary wrote charming letters on full-size sheets folded over without an envelope and sealed in black wax with a carved Greek seal. "I never was more shocked than by Miss Eaton's . . . appearance," reads one witty little note. "I never saw a woman so changed, and the faces she makes when singing put one in mind of a cat trying to swallow a bone." But this deliberately casual approach did not keep Payne from declaring his love, and in 1825 he asked Mary to marry him.

Mary was firm but tactful. Having been Shelley's wife, she knew none but a man of equal genius could satisfy her. The only man she might have considered was Washington Irving—at that time his fame was greater than Shelley's—but although Payne loved her so unselfishly that he tried to promote a romance between her and Irving, nothing much came of it. Irving was cautious, and once Mary wrote wryly that if, indeed, she and Irving were ever married, it would be when the "Bride and Bridegroom's joint ages amounted to the discreet number of 145 and 3 months."

Mary's next suitor was far more impetuous. He was Prosper Mérimée, the young French poet and novelist who wrote *Carmen*, the melodrama on which the famous opera is based. Mérimée was several years her junior, and Mary was flattered and amused by his interest, particularly since he fell in love with her while she was recuperating from smallpox—a disease that left her pretty skin—fortunately only temporarily—pitted. "What will you say also to the imagination of one of the cleverest men in France, young and a poet, who could be interested in me in spite of the marks I wore?" she reported to a friend. To Mérimée's proposal she replied that since she was not a flirt, she was returning his letter; she thought that at some later time he might regret having written it.

The most serious of Mary's suitors was Trelawney. Trelawney was a vivid figure. Mary described him when they first met in Italy as "partly natural and partly perhaps put on." His appearance, she wrote, was "oriental"; he was dark-haired and well built, with a warm smile that assured her that "his heart is good." Mary liked his tall tales about his adventures, too. She was "glad to meet with one who, among other valuable qualities, has the rare merit of interesting my imagination."

Throughout the years of her widowhood, Mary kept a friendship with Trelawney—no easy feat, because Trelawney wanted material for a life of Shelley, and Mary refused to anger Sir Timothy and risk her boy's small allowance. But Mary made up for it by helping to place Trelawney's book *The Adventures of a*

Younger Son. Her letters were light and joking; she teased him about his women friends who had married by telling him that if she or Claire were to die or marry, he would be left without a woman admirer at all!

Trelawney's answer surprised her: "Do not you, dear Mary, abandon me by following the evil examples of my other ladies. I should not wonder if fate, without our choice, united us; and who can control his fate?"

Mary recognized that Trelawney was proposing marriage, but rather than turn him down cold, she did it gracefully. "Mary Shelley shall be written on my tomb—and why?" she wrote him. "I cannot tell, except that it is so pretty a name that . . . I should never have the heart to get rid of it."

Trelawney was accustomed to success with women. Mary's rejection made him more persistent. "Trelawney too is a good name, and sounds as well as Shelley," he wrote.

Mary, now alarmed, had no choice except to speak straightforwardly. "My name will *never* be Trelawney," she wrote, underlining the "never" several times.

I am not so young as I was when you first knew me, but I am as proud. I must have the entire affection, devotion, and, above all, the solicitous protection of any one who would win me. You belong to womenkind in general, and Mary Shelley will *never* be yours.

While her romantic life occupied only a small part of her thoughts, Mary's professional life continued to expand. She had made the right decision about Trelawney, she thought. In the summer of 1832—a year after she told him she would not marry him—Mary described Trelawney in her diary as "a strange yet wonderful being—endued with genius—great force of character and power of feeling—but destroyed by *being nothing*—destroyed by envy and internal dissatisfaction." In taking on new challenges, Mary vowed she never would become *nothing* herself.

Partly because she liked literary criticism and history, and partly because the work was steady and profitable, Mary began to write essays for Lardner's *Cabinet Cyclopaedia* on a wide range of subjects—from Dante and Cervantes to minor, and now forgotten, Italian poets. In 1830 she completed another novel, *The Fortunes of Perkin Warbeck*, and although she was disappointed in its sale—"only 150 pounds for poor Perkin Warbeck," she wrote—she shortly began another, titled *Lodore*.

Money was still the problem. Although Shelley's eldest son, Charles (Harriet's boy), died suddenly in 1826, making Percy Florence heir to the family title and fortune, neither Mary nor Percy would realize anything much until Sir Timothy died. If Percy was to have the education his mother intended, it was she who would have to send him to Harrow. Mary figured her assets and budgeted as best she could. Finally she made a hard decision: She would give up her home in London and take inexpensive lodgings in Harrow in order to be close to Percy and to save money.

She hated Harrow. It was stodgy, conservative, a small town. "I like society," she wrote. "I believe all persons who have any talent (who are in good health) do." London was alive with theater, music, a home to the brightest and best intellects and wits in England. There Mary had a lively social circle: her own friends such as Thomas Moore, the Irish poet; Julia and Isabel Robinson, close women friends; and her father's long-time companions whom she had known from child-hood. "Debarred from that," she wrote, "how I have pined and died."

Actually she did nothing of the sort. With friends and stimulation she was less inclined to introspection; now, left to her own resources, she made a companion of herself—the child she had been, and the young woman. She put her memories and experience into *Lodore*, the novel she wrote at Harrow. "Have you read *Lodore*?" Mary wrote to a friend in 1835. "If you did read it, did you recognize any of Shelley's and my early adventures—when we were in danger of being starved in Switzerland—and could get no dinner at an inn in London." In *Lodore*, the character of Ethel is based on Mary's own life, while Shelley appears in part in three of the male characters. Even Shelley's entries in their joint journal were used in the novel. Ethel is described as "insensible to all future evil. She feels as if our love would alone suffice to resist the invasions of calamity"—the very phrases Shelley wrote in the first days of their elopement!

Mary's recreating of her years with Shelley in *Lodore* was one way of escaping her loneliness. The other solace was Percy.

Mary's son suited her fine. All her life she had lived among genius, and her son, a throwback to the stolid, calm, good-natured country squires of Sussex, Shel-ley's ancestors, soothed her soul. Percy was a nice-looking, even-tempered boy: "He gets on very well—and is a fine boy . . ." Mary wrote "This hot weather, though he exposes himself to the sun—instead of making him languid, heightens the color in his cheeks and brightens his eyes. He is always gay and in good humour—which is a great blessing."

But even more than from her pleasure in her boy, or in her writing, the peace Mary eventually found at Harrow came from reliance on *herself*. By the time Percy Florence was sixteen, she was able to send him to board with a tutor in preparation for his entrance into Cambridge University, and she was now finally alone. In the thirteen years since Shelley's death, she had found success in her profession, made new friends and lost old ones, reared her son by herself, taken on the financial support of her aging father, faced illness and the fading of her beauty. Now, at the beginning of her middle age, she had the knowledge that she had somehow, against all odds, survived. The years at Harrow and the loneliness had toughened her and made her self-sufficient. "I am more wrapt up in myself, my own feelings . . . and prospects for Percy. I am now proof, as Hamlet says, both against man and woman," she wrote to her friend Trelawney.

In her diary, in the last entry she was to make for four years, she wrote in relief and nostalgic longing, "My race is run."

10

"An Unreal Phantasmagoria"

Even as a girl, brooding and dreaming in the heather-fragrant hills of Scotland, Mary was introspective. As she grew into womanhood she developed social grace and poise, but the long-time habit of looking inward persisted. In her later years her friendships dimmed; she confided only in her diary, setting her priorities in order, tallying up her life.

Her first order of duty, Mary thought, was raising Percy Florence. She was determined that Percy was not to suffer because he was half orphaned, so she resigned herself to writing popular fiction that would sell well. In fact, once when Claire told her, "You could write upon metaphysics, politics, jurisprudence, astronomy, mathematics—all those highest subjects which men taunt us with being incapable of treating—and surpass them," Mary simply reminded

Claire that she had a son dependent upon her. Mary succeeded well enough to send Percy to a fine prep school and to one of the most distinguished universities in England.

Her real life's work Mary saw as editing and publishing Shelley's poetry. At the time of his death, Shelley was considered "a minor poet married to a major novelist." It was through Mary's efforts and devotion that he finally received, after his death, the recognition that she thought he deserved. The irony of Mary's life was that while Shelley's work would reach only an educated minority, *Frankenstein* would remain timelessly popular, widely read, and viewed in all the media by untold millions. Mary never visualized this outcome, nor is there any reason to believe she would have cared very much. There is little mention of her work in her letters and journals. Whatever her problems were with "invention," as she called her imagination, they were given short shrift. Her diary and correspondence describe her daily life, her efforts to provide for her son, her progress with publishers in placing Shelley's poetry and prose before the public, her loneliness, valiant courage, at last the triumph over obstacles and the attainment of a measure of serenity and peace.

Mary's last tragedy was the death of her father on April 7, 1836. Unlike the other losses in her life, this one was bearable. Godwin, for whom she had felt such an overpowering love in her childhood, had fallen off his pedestal later in her life, but as long as he was alive, Mary felt a strong sense of obligation to him, and even after his death to his widow, her difficult and quarrelsome stepmother. Mary had arranged for a job for her father some years earlier as Yeoman Usher of the Exchequer at two hundred pounds a year. Now that he was gone, she petitioned successfully for a pension for Mrs. Godwin. Then, her conscience absolutely clear, she closed the book.

Godwin had left his unpublished manuscript *The Genius of Christianity Unveiled* for Mary to edit and publish. Resolutely she put it in a trunk, where it remained, unpublished, for twenty years after her death. Her father was gone, she reasoned, and her duty was ended. Her loyalty belonged to her son. Godwin's atheistic last manuscript would have brought down the wrath of Sir Timothy—at the very time that, as she wrote in a letter to a friend, she had

> to fight my poor Percy's battle—to try to get him sent to College without further dilapidation of his ruined prospects . . . that this should be undertaken at a moment when a cry was raised against his Mother—and that not on the question of *politics* but *religion*—would mar all— I must see him fairly launched, before I commit myself to the fury of the waves.

Mary's own life had required so much strength of will that she had short patience with the popular "Byronic" view of life; the romantic "weltschmerz," or world-weariness, Mary called an "impatience of life under sorrow, suicide in despair." Stoically, Mary maintained that "to feel that adversity and prosperity are both lessons to teach us a higher wisdom . . . ought to be the aim of every writer." Her last novel, *Falkner*, published in 1837, expands upon that theme.

Like all of Mary's books, *Falkner* made money for

her. This one finally relieved some anxiety about the future, and she knew when she finished it that it was the last yarn she would spin. Time, she thought, was running out; she now had to turn with all her energies once again to making the world see Shelley as she had seen him.

Time and again Mary had been stopped by Sir Timothy's prohibitions from her early plan to write Shelley's biography. As a compromise between what she wanted and what she thought Shelley's father would allow, she gathered and edited and printed a volume, *Posthumous Poems*, in 1824. Her careful balance on the tightrope wasn't good enough; Sir Timothy objected, and the edition was recalled. Mary took it in stride: Sir Timothy would soon die—how much longer could he live? she wondered—and then she could do what she wanted.

Sir Timothy lived into his nineties—Mary eventually wryly called him "Old Time"—but gradually he mellowed, while Mary grew smarter about handling him. When in 1835 Edward Moxon offered her six hundred pounds for an edition of Shelley's poetry, she seriously considered it. She wrote to Hogg in 1838, "Sir Timothy forbids Biography under threat of stopping the supplies. . . . How could I live? But I mean to write a few Notes appertaining to the history of the Poems." Summoning all her tact, Mary managed to achieve her purpose without violating Sir Timothy's wishes. Four volumes of *Shelley's Poetical Works* came out in 1839. While Shelley was still controversial—the publisher was sued in 1841 for "blasphemous libel" in including *Queen Mab*, and the next edition appeared without certain passages of the atheistic poem—reviewers praised the edition. At last Shelley was recognized as the great poet he was!

Shelley's prose works were published in 1840, along with a new edition of *A History of a Six Weeks' Tour*—the little volume that Mary and Shelley had written together the summer they eloped. Later that year Percy came of age, and Mary used the money she had earned from Shelley's poems and prose to take the boy abroad. In the company of her beloved son and two of his friends, Mary was happier than she had been in years. On June 1 she wrote in her diary:

> I must mark this evening, tired as I am, for it's one among few—soothing and balmy. Long oppressed by care, disappointment, and ill health, which all combined to depress and irritate me, I feel almost to have lost the spring of happy reverie. On such a night it returns—the calm sea, the soft breeze, the silver moon new bent in the western heaven—nature in her sweetest mood, raises one's thoughts to God and imparted peace.
>
> Indeed, I have many, many blessings. . . . If I could restore health, administer balm to the wounded heart, and banish care from those I love, I were in myself happy, while I am loved and Percy continues the blessing that he is. Still, who on such a night must not feel the weight of sorrow lessened? For myself, I repose in gentle and grateful reverie, and hope for others. I am content for myself. Years have—how much!—cooled the ardent and swift spirit that at such hours bore me freely along. Yet, though I no longer soar, I

repose. Though I no longer deem all things attainable, I enjoy what is, and while I feel that whatever I have lost of youth and hope, I have acquired the enduring affection of a noble heart, and Percy shows such excellent dispositions that I feel I am much the gainer in life.

God and good angels guard us! surely this world, stored outwardly with shapes and influences of beauty and good, is peopled in its intellectual life by myriads of loving spirits that mould our thoughts to the good. . . . Such surely gather round one on such an evening, and make part of that atmosphere of love, so hushed, so soft, on which the soul reposes and is blest.

On this tranquil note, Mary's diary ends forever. Life, so long a test and a trial, now held only happy occasions and beautiful memories. The trip abroad retraced her travels with Shelley, and she writes poignantly in *Rambles in Germany and Italy*:

At length I caught a glimpse of the scenes among which I had lived, when I first stepped out from childhood into life. There, on the shores of Bellerive stood Diodati; and our humbler dwelling Maison Chapuis, nestled close to the lake below. There were the terraces, the vineyards, the upward path threading them, the little port where our boat lay moored; I could mark and recognize a thousand slight peculiarities, familiar objects then—forgotten then—forgotten since—now replete with recollections and associations. Was I the same person who had lived there, the companion of the dead? For all were gone; even my young child, whom I had looked upon as the joy of future years, had died in infancy—not one hope, then in fair bud, had opened to maturity; storm and blight and death had passed over, and destroyed all. While yet very young, I had reached the position of an aged person.

Here Byron, magnificent in exile, and Shelley, radiant in his hopes and visions, had talked through the night at the fireside of Villa Diodati. Here Mary and Shelley had floated on the calm lake, watching the sun set behind the mountains. Here, in Mary's moonlit bedroom, Frankenstein's Monster had emerged from her "waking dream. . . . All my life since was but an unreal phantasmagoria," Mary wrote; "the shades that gathered round that scene were the realities."

In April 1844 Sir Timothy died, "falling from the stalk like an overblown flower," Mary told Hogg. Percy succeeded to the baronetcy, and Mary came into a comfortable legacy—as did Claire, under Shelley's will. A few years later Percy met and married Jane St. John, a young widow whom Mary described as "a prize indeed in the lottery, being the best and sweetest thing in the world."

Mary, Percy, and Jane returned to Field Place to live out their lives in Shelley's boyhood home. "Jane dislikes society and Percy has the same tastes— We have our garden and our farm." Once Claire descended from Paris, but Jane, truly Mary's kindred spirit, made short work of her. "She has been the bane of my existence ever since I was three," Mary explained, while Jane made graceful excuses and bustled

Claire back to France. Mary's years were spent in peace and solitude, tended by the son and daughter-in-law who loved and understood her, until at last on February 1, 1851, when she was fifty-four years old, her brave heart gave out and she was quietly laid to rest.

11

Frankenstein in the Twentieth Century

Mary's Monster has survived her by more than a century. While Mary's sojourn ended in 1851, her scientist and his nameless creation have continued their voyage into the twentieth century, translating themselves from the novel to plays, to movies, and to television, changing form chameleon fashion to accommodate each age's visions of horror.

Generation after generation, with no idea who Mary Shelley was, is still fascinated, lining up to see the latest in the continuing stream of theatrical and motion picture productions. Untold millions have quaked in fear at Victor Frankenstein's gruesome grave robbing, have recoiled in terror at the murder of Frankenstein's brother, friend, and bride. Breathlessly they have followed the Fiend's bloody trail through the gloomy mountain passes and over icy

Arctic wastelands as the scientist presses ever onward to rid the world of the abomination he created. More than one hundred and fifty years after its original publication, the book remains in print in every major European and Oriental language, and its name has become a household word. The history of *Frankenstein* is unique in literature, and its author—strangely unknown—continues to occupy a place among the most important prophetic writers of all times.

Frankenstein's voyage began with its anonymous publication in 1818. The book was rejected by the first publisher to whom Mary submitted it, and the firm that finally put it into print did not foresee a bestseller. But the book sold well, and a further unaltered edition appeared in 1823. Within the next few years it had aroused enough interest to be tapped for a well-known series called "Standard Novels." The first of these included an introduction by Mary. The book was reprinted in 1839, and again in 1849.

Six subsequent editions of Mary's first novel appear in the British Museum Catalogue during the period of her lifetime, and there were other, cheap editions which were unlisted. At least seven further editions have been published in the United States between 1845 and 1949, with countless editions in paperback, abridged and condensed versions in anthologies, and even comic-strip editions. Since the first year of its publication there has always been, somewhere in the world, a printing press at work turning out still another copy or version of Mary's immortal story.

As a play, too, the story was an immediate sensation: "Terrific!" "Mysterious!" promised the playbills and advertisements of the 1820's. The first version, *Presumption, or the Fate of Frankenstein*, opened at the English Opera House on July 28, 1823. Mary, a member of the audience, was "amused" by Thomas Potter Cooke, who stole the show as the unnamed Monster. Cooke was the Boris Karloff of his day. "He powerfully embodied the horrible," said *The Drama*, a periodical of the time, "bordering on the sublime and the awful." Cooke, as later actors were to do, invented his own makeup. From one magazine we get a description: His face was streaked with green and yellow makeup, his long, matted, straggling black locks hung loose, his arms and legs were painted blue, his mouth was a straight black gash.

The dramatic possibilities of *Frankenstein* were quickly seen. At the same time that *Presumption, or the Fate of Frankenstein* appeared, another quite different version, *Frankenstein, or the Demon of Switzerland*, by H. M. Milner, was staged at the Coburg Theatre. A further seal of fame was provided by a parody—this one referring to the new steam age—*Frank in Steam, or the Modern Promise to Pay*. Other burlesques on Mary's theme occur in London stage records from 1840 to 1887.

Twentieth-century media had barely emerged before they explored the infinite possible variations on the *Frankenstein* story. In 1910, using a hand-crank camera, the Edison Stock Company filmed a Brillo-haired actor named Charles Ogle as the Monster. The film, which ran barely ten minutes, portrayed the scientist as a young student who became absorbed in the secrets of life and death. Press releases on the film described the creation of the Monster in a "cauldron of blazing chemicals," as opposed to the later-day use of electrical energy.

Electrical pyrotechnics—zigzags of manmade lightning, an electrically lighted and powered laboratory, life coming from electrical "charges" emanating from a giant dynamo—were the background to the first important Frankenstein film, the version starring Boris Karloff as the Monster and Colin Clive as the scientist. The movie, which was made in 1931, is a perfect representative of the time in which it was made. The technology of the '30's was typified by a major exhibit at the 1939 New York World's Fair: A giant robot, given "instructions" through a microphone, previewed the birth of computer cybernetics.

Boris Karloff, in the role of the Monster, reflects the motorized robot into which the character evolved. The Fiend was no longer a grotesquerie of graveyard parts. Karloff's makeup—which he copyrighted—delineated a motorized Monster, complete even to the clips and electrodes in his head and neck.

The public's reaction to the first of the Karloff *Frankenstein* films was so overwhelmingly enthusiastic that the film industry immediately recognized a winner. *Frankenstein* was followed by *The Bride of Frankenstein*. This film (in which, incidentally, the name "Frankenstein" is misused to mean the Monster, instead of his creator—a practice that continued throughout the later versions) spawned *Son of Frankenstein*, *The Ghost of Frankenstein*, *Frankenstein Meets the Wolf Man*, and *House of Frankenstein*. These starred, in order: Karloff, Lon Chaney, Jr., Bela Lugosi, and Glenn Strange. Reverting again to its early adaptation to satire, the Frankenstein theme was again used, however peripherally, in *Abbott and Costello Meet Frankenstein*. It was successfully modified to appeal to a huge new teenage audience—the children of the Second World War's baby boom—in *I Was a Teenage Frankenstein* (with the Monster sporting a T-shirt and Ivy League slacks) and a 1957 film futuristically titled *Frankenstein—1970*.

The 1950's brought a new series that mined the Frankenstein ore: *The Curse of Frankenstein 1957*, followed by such offshoots as *The Revenge of Frankenstein* and *Frankenstein Creates Woman*. Frankenstein entered the world of pop art in Andy Warhol's *Frankenstein*, and the realm of pure comedy in Mel Brooks' brilliant takeoff, *Young Frankenstein*. Through satire, Mel Brooks extracts the very essence of Mary's story: "Love is the only thing that can save this poor creature, and I am going to convince him that he is loved, even at the cost of my own life," cries Frederick Frankenstein, grandson of the Monster's original creator, in a hilarious scene. "This is a nice boy, this is a good boy, this is a mother's angel," the young scientist croons to the yearning Monster, "I want the world to know once and for all without any shame that we love him!" The redeeming power of love, as Mary herself indicated, was the only way to undo the curse of Frankenstein's creation.

Television, being a medium of "reality" rather than of illusion like films and the theater, used the Frankenstein story in its own way. The most elaborate of the films, NBC's 1973 television movie *Frankenstein: The True Story*, sets Mary's tale within a frame of biography. The production, which featured a screenplay by Christopher Isherwood and Don Bachardy, performances by Leonard Whiting and James Mason, and cameo appearances by Sir Ralph Richardson and Sir John Gielgud, was meant as a serious return to what the screenplay's credits call "a classic novel by Mary W. Shelley." The play, however, despite the fact that it opens with a scene in which Mary Shelley, Byron, Shelley, and Polidori are picnicking beside a Swiss lake, takes considerable liberties with Mary's story.

In the second ambitious television treatment, this one produced on ABC-TV the same year, much more fidelity to the original novel is maintained. The Dan Curtis production of *Frankenstein*, which was shown on two successive nights in 1973 as part of the series *Wide World of Entertainment*, was written by Sam Hall and Richard Landau. In this production the geography of the story is abbreviated, but the names and personalities of all but the Monster are kept intact. The Monster is called the Giant and is portrayed as a powerful but innocent "giant baby." True to Mary's concept, though, the scientist is a sensitive and sympathetic idealist who errs through his own arrogance.

While Mary's story was grist for the new media of the twentieth century—television, radio, and the motion pictures—it was also responsible for the creation of a new form in an old medium: literature. Scholars who trace science fiction to its source inevitably name *Frankenstein* and Mary Shelley. In his chapter entitled "The Origins of the Species: Mary Shelley," which appears in *Billion Year Spree*, author Brian W. Aldiss defines science fiction in these words: "Science fiction is the search for a definition of man and his status in the universe which will stand in our advanced scientific state of knowledge, and is characteristically cast in the Gothic or post-Gothic mould." In other words, while science fiction uses the mood of Gothic stories—a sense of impending doom, horror, the supernatural, and even sometimes the trappings of the Gothic novel, such as gloomy woods, haunted castles, hooting owls, and so on—the predicament that the protagonists face must be one brought about by science. Evolution run wild, invasions from as yet unexplored planets, the creation of life by a mortal—these are science-fiction problems.

From its genesis in Mary's *Frankenstein*, scholars in the field of science fiction trace the development of science fiction in subsequent writings by Edgar Allan Poe, Robert Louis Stevenson's *The Strange Case of Dr. Jekyll and Mr. Hyde*, the novels of H. G. Wells—most specifically *The Island of Dr. Moreau*—through today's "mad scientists" in books by Ray Bradbury, Robert A. Heinlein, and other masters of the genre. The very word "robot" was coined by Karel Čapek from the Czech root meaning "work." Čapek's play *R.U.R.*, the first work in which an android robot appears, is the embodiment of the author's fears that increasing automation and regimentation would dehumanize mankind. The protagonist has invented a formula whereby artificial people can be made in a factory. Victor Frankenstein's solitary creation has now, in the twentieth century, become the product of a conveyer belt—a conclusion that Aldiss calls the "logical development of the Frankenstein theme."

Books, movies, plays, radio, and television—all the sources of amusement with which we are familiar—have been immeasurably enriched by Mary's waking dream. But if *Frankenstein* were only an entertainment, it would long since have been forgotten, become a dusty period piece like so many other narratives that have captured the attention of one generation or another. It was Mary Shelley's prophecy of the future, a gift rooted in her uncanny ability to extract the essence of the past and her present in order to forecast the future, that has made *Frankenstein* a classic, as valid in our times as in Mary's. Mary differed from the Romantics who, seeing the abuses of science, looked backward yearningly toward the idealized "noble savage," unencumbered by the complexities of modern existence, a simple child of nature, serene and peaceful in being at one with a benevolent universe. She parted from the utilitarians, who saw science as salvation and its failings as being somewhat like warts on a healthy body—flaws that could be removed while leaving the whole intact. Mary was the first writer to see science and progress as essentially neutral, containing within themselves, rather than as a result of their abuses, the seeds of evil as well as good.

Mary Shelley's relevance to our time and place was perhaps best summed up by her biographer Elizabeth Nitchie:

> Frankenstein's motives were not pure research. He saw himself as the benefactor of the world, creating a new and happy species and even restoring the dead to life. Instead he had created a monstrosity and brought death to the living. We hear almost daily in this atomic age the mourning voice of the scientist speaking the words of Frankenstein: Alas, I had turned loose into the world a depraved wretch, whose delight was in carnage and misery: Has he not murdered my Brother?

And the creature used for destruction warns, You are my creator, but I am your master.

The gap between the promise of science to improve the quality of life and its performance has lengthened since Mary sounded her warning. In the century and a half since *Frankenstein* first appeared, Mary's Monster has become more than ever a symbol for the problem that perplexes our generation: *What is humanity to do with science, technology, and the power to alter and create life itself?*

Today technology and industry insure that workers need not labor from dawn to dark in sweat shops. Child labor laws, compensation, hour-and-wage regulations, standards for hygiene and safety, all have become part of modern industrial life. But what of the effect of mass industry upon the environment? The dangers of air pollution, the dangers of destroying the ecological balance, of despoiling the seas and rivers? All these spinoffs of scientific and industrial progress threaten life itself on this planet.

Mary's mentor, Dr. Erasmus Darwin, has fallen into obscurity, eclipsed by his grandson, Charles Darwin who, in *The Origin of Species*, gave the world the theory of evolution that provides the foundation for the entire structure of modern biology. On their most basic level, Darwin's theories tell us that change is the rule of the universe and the law of life. The common framework of ideas he provided linked together the scattered details of botany, zoology, physiology and medicine, anatomy and behavior. Through Darwinian theories and those of Gregor Mendel, his contemporary, scientists have benefited the world's food supply, have made important breakthroughs toward solving the riddle of inherited diseases. But the dark side of science, too, has emerged. Darwinian and Mendelian theories have been used to justify disastrously unhumanistic experiments in "selective breeding" and sterilization of "genetically inferior" races and people. Hitler's rationale for the elimination of "racial undesirables" may be seen as a pseudoscientific application of Darwinism. More recently, there have been those who have misused Darwinism to evaluate intelligence on the basis of racial and ethnic background.

Mary's Monster was fabricated from the organs of corpses. Modern science has turned Mary's nightmare into a promised dream, in the use of organ transplants to restore sight to the blind, to transfer hearts and kidneys from the recently dead to the living. But what of the ethics of death-into-life? The genius of medical science has been presented with questions never before faced: What actually constitutes life? Is it a heartbeat? Respiration? Brain function? Under what conditions should life be restored? Prolonged? Terminated? And who should arbitrate these dilemmas? Is it in the province of religion? Law? Government?

These questions have been brought to the fore in a dramatic way with the birth of the first "test-tube baby"—Louise Brown, in Oldham, England, on July 25, 1978. Louise's conception was the outcome of years of medical experimentation. It was accomplished by taking an egg cell from the mother through an incision in the woman's abdomen, fertilizing the egg with the husband's sperm and maintaining the result in a nutrient broth in a culture dish for about two days, and then introducing the resulting embryo, by means of a plastic tube through the vaginal canal and cervix, into the uterus, where it was implanted on the mother's uterine wall. But as intricate as the medical procedure is, the ethical and moral problems are even more complex.

Bioethicists—a growing core of concerned scientists who deal with the moral issues in science, along with lawyers, researchers, and theologians—are beginning to tangle with such troubling issues as these: Will embryo implant lead to the use of paid surrogate mothers—women who are engaged for a fee to carry the embryo to birth? If so, who has legal rights if the surrogate mother refuses to turn over the baby? What about undiscovered genetic damage? How would we know whether manipulation of the embryo during the implant would lead to genetic damage that may not surface for years? What about the rights of the fetus? If the embryo is abnormal or damaged should it be destroyed? Or would it be a person—entitled to legal protection?

The scientific realities of our day have come so close to Mary's prophecy that reality, not fantasy, brings shivers of anticipation, makes the blood run cold. In this last quarter of the twentieth century, our own scientists have, indeed, found the power to create life itself. What would Mary have made of a newspaper headline in 1978 that announced: LISTEN FRANKENSTEIN: LAB-LIFE IS PATENTABLE. Or the story it describes—the first court decision specifically authorizing a patent for a life form created in a laboratory. It is a bacterium altered by implanting bits of new genetic code material from other strains of bacteria in order to better consume spilled oil.

What, indeed, would an eighteen-year-old girl, arising from her waking dream in her remote cottage in the Swiss Alps more than a century and a half ago, have thought about the scientific debate that has surrounded genetics research—a scientific and moral problem so pressing that it has called forth a stringent list of regulations and guidelines established by the National Institute of Health in 1978? The dilemma, which was examined in heated debate at a meeting of the International Conference on Recombinant DNA Molecules—a convocation of 156 scientists from the Soviet Union, Japan, Australia, Israel, the United States, and ten European countries—is about the possible benefits and dangers of what has been called the most important scientific breakthrough of this century, the recombinant DNA techniques which allow biologists to "stitch together" gene segments from two unrelated organisms.

The gain from such knowledge may be immeasurable: It may hold the key to a permanent solution of the problem of food supply for an increasing population by creating major food crops with the ability to convert atmospheric nitrogen to fertilizer. It may hold the clue to elimination of genetic disease, possibly including some forms of cancer. But scientists are unable to measure the risks of such knowledge. A single unrecognized accident could contaminate the entire earth with a dangerous and ineradicable agent that might not reveal its presence until its deadly work was done, for results of the experiment are unlike other potentially dangerous substances. If we stop manufacturing DDT or Red Dye No. 2, they will in time cease to be problems. But the altered bacteria are *alive*, and as Horace Judson, in his article "Fearful of Science" (*Harper's Magazine*, June 1975), writes: "The nastiest novelty of all these biological hazards is that *they are living creatures, able to multiply.*" The problem is so chillingly close to Dr. Frankenstein's that one can almost hear Mary's scientist's anguished cry: "But what if a race of devils would be propagated upon the earth who might make the very existence of the species of man a condition precarious and full of terror?"

"'So much has been done,' exclaimed the soul of Frankenstein; 'more, far more will I achieve.'" In the more than one hundred and fifty years since Mary Shelley wrote her prophetic novel, humanity has solved the riddle of matter, harnessed the atom to our service, explored the solar system, sent missiles to Mars, and landed men on the moon. And yet, still, the question she posed in 1816 remains unanswered. Science and knowledge are in themselves neither a destructive force nor one for salvation. It is our ability to use them for love, for humanity, that is the promise of a better life. To what uses will we put our power to create and destroy—to make a world in which beauty, love, and justice triumph, or one in which life itself becomes monstrous?

It is the most important challenge of our time.

Chronology

1757 Birth of William Godwin, Mary's father
1759 Birth of Mary Wollstonecraft, Mary's mother,
     April 21
1792 Birth of Percy Bysshe Shelley, August 4
1794 Birth of Fanny Imlay, Mary's half-sister, May
1797 Marriage of William Godwin and Mary
     Wollstonecraft, March
     Birth of Mary Wollstonecraft Godwin (Shelley),
     August 30
     Death of Mary's mother, September 10
1811 Marriage of Percy Bysshe Shelley and Harriet
     Westbrook
1812 Mary's first meeting with Shelley and Harriet,
     November 11
1814 Mary's meeting with Shelley, May 5
     Mary and Shelley's elopement, July 28
     Mary and Shelley return to England, September 14
1815 Birth of Mary and Shelley's daughter, February 22
     Death of daughter, March 6
1816 Birth of son, William, January 24
     Residence in Switzerland, May–August
     Return to England, August 29

Fanny Imlay commits suicide, October 9

Harriet Shelley found drowned, December 10

1817 Birth of Allegra, daughter of Claire Clairmont and
Byron, January 12

Residence in Marlow, March 1817–March 1818

History of a Six Weeks' Tour published

Birth of daughter, Clara Everina, September 2

1818 *Frankenstein* published, March 11

Departure for Italy, March 11

Death of Clara in Venice, September 24

1819 Death of William in Rome, June 7

Birth of son, Percy Florence, in Florence, November 12

1821 Arrival of Edward and Jane Williams, January 16

Arrival of Byron, November 1

1822 Arrival of Trelawney, January 14

Death of Allegra, April 19

Miscarriage, June 16

Arrival of Hunts in Leghorn, June

Drowning of Shelley and Williams, July 8

1823 Publication of *Valperga*

Return to England, August 25

1824 Publication of Shelley's *Posthumous Poems*

Death of Byron, April 19

1826 Publication of *The Last Man*

Death of Harriet's son, Charles Bysshe, making
Percy Florence heir to the title, September 14

1830 Publication of *Perkin Warbeck*

1833 Residence in Harrow

1835 Publication of *Lodore*

1836 Death of Godwin, April 7

1837 Publication of *Falkner*

1839 Publication of Shelley's *Poetical Works*

Publication of Shelley's *Essays, Letters from Abroad,
Translations and Fragments* (dated 1840)

1840 First trip on continent with Percy and his friends
1842– Second trip on continent with Percy and his
43   friends
1844 Publication of *Rambles in Germany and Italy*
     Death of Sir Timothy Shelley
1848 Marriage of Percy Florence and Jane St. John,
     June 22
1851 Death of Mary Shelley, February 1

Frankenstein on Film

1910 *Frankenstein.* Edison, USA. A one-reel version featuring Charles Ogle, a member of the Edison stock company.

1915 *Life Without Soul.* Ocean Film Company, USA. A five-reel version of the story featuring the English actor Percy Standing.

1931 *Frankenstein.* Universal, USA. Directed by James Whale. Produced by Carl Laemmle. Adapted from a play by Peggy Webling. Screenplay by Garrett Fort and Francis Edward Faragoh (adaptation by John L. Balderston). Boris Karloff as the Monster, Colin Clive as Dr. Henry Frankenstein.

1935 *Bride of Frankenstein.* Universal, USA. Directed by James Whale. Produced by Carl Laemmle. Screenplay by John L. Balderston. Boris Karloff again played the Monster and Colin Clive Henry Frankenstein. Elsa Lanchester was the bride of the film's title.

1939 *The Son of Frankenstein.* Universal, USA. Directed by Rowland V. Lee. Produced by Rowland V. Lee. Screenplay by Willis Cooper. Basil Rathbone was

Baron Wolfgang von Frankenstein and Karloff the Monster.

1942 *The Ghost of Frankenstein.* Universal, USA. Directed by Erle C. Kenton. Produced by George Waggner. Screenplay by W. Scott Darling based on an original story by Eric Taylor. Sir Cedric Hardwicke was Dr. Ludwig Frankenstein and Lon Chaney, Jr., portrayed the Monster. Bela Lugosi played Ygor.

1943 *Frankenstein Meets the Wolf Man.* Universal, USA. Directed by Roy William Neil. Produced by George Waggner. Screenplay by Curt Siodmak. Bela Lugosi portrayed the Monster. Lon Chaney, Jr., played the Wolf Man.

1944 *The House of Frankenstein.* Universal, USA. Directed by Erle C. Kenton. Produced by Paul Malvern. Screenplay by Edward T. Lowe. Karloff played a mad doctor, Lon Chaney, Jr., the Wolf Man, John Carradine was Dracula, J. Carrol Naish was a murderous hunchback, and Glenn Strange became the Frankenstein Monster.

1945 *House of Dracula.* Universal, USA. Directed by Erle C. Kenton. Produced by Paul Malvern. Screenplay by Edward T. Lowe based on a story by George Bricker and Dwight V. Babcock. Lon Chaney, Jr., as the Wolf Man, John Carradine as Dracula, Onslow Stevens as the mad doctor, Jane Adams as a hunchback, and Glenn Strange as the Monster.

1948 *Abbott and Costello Meet Frankenstein.* Universal, USA. Directed by Charles T. Barton. Produced by Robert Arthur. Screenplay by Robert Lees, Frederic Rinaldo, and John Grant. Lon Chaney, Jr., was the Wolf Man, Bela Lugosi returned to the screen as Dracula, and Glenn Strange played the Monster.

1957 *The Curse of Frankenstein.* Hammer Films, Great Britain. Directed by Terence Fisher. Produced by Anthony Hinds. Executive Producer Michael Carreras. Associate Producer, Anthony Nelson-Keyes. Screenplay by Jimmy Sangster. The first color production of the famous tale. Peter Cushing was Baron Victor Frankenstein, and his monstrous creation was portrayed by Christopher Lee.

1957 *I Was a Teenage Frankenstein.* American-International, USA. Directed by Herbert L. Stock. Produced by Herman Cohen. Story and screenplay by Kenneth Langtry. Whit Bissell was Professor Frankenstein, and Gary Conway the Monster created from the parts of dead teenagers.

1958 *Frankenstein—1970.* Allied Artists, USA. Directed by Howard W. Koch. Produced by Aubrey Schenck. Screenplay by Richard Landau and George Worthing Yates, based on a story by Aubrey Schenck and Charles A. Moses. Boris Karloff played the disfigured Victor Frankenstein, a victim of Nazi torture, who brings back his ancestor's earlier creation by means of an atomic device.

1958 *The Revenge of Frankenstein.* Hammer Films, Great Britain. Directed by Terence Fisher. Produced by Anthony Hinds. Executive Producer, Michael Carreras. Associate Producer, Anthony Nelson-Keyes. Screenplay by Jimmy Sangster, with additional dialogue by H. Hurford Janes.

1959 *Frankenstein's Daughter.* Astor Pictures, USA. Directed by Richard Cunha. Produced by Marc Frederic. Screenplay by H. E. Barrie. John Ashley played John Bruder (supposedly the son of Frankenstein), who created Sandra Knight as his Monster.

1964 *The Evil of Frankenstein.* Hammer Films, Great Britain, Directed by Freddie Francis. Produced by Anthony Hinds. Screenplay by John Elder (Anthony Hinds). Peter Cushing as Baron Frankenstein creating a new monstrosity, played by Kiwi Kingston.

1965 *Frankenstein Meets the Space Monster.* Vernon Films, USA (released in Great Britain as *Duel of the Space Monsters*). Directed by Robert Gaffney. In the cast were Robert Reilly, Jim Karen, and Nancy Marshall.

1965 *Jesse James Meets Frankenstein's Daughter.* Embassy Pictures, USA. Directed by William Beaudine. Produced by Carroll Case. Story and screenplay by Carl H. Hittleman.

1967 *Frankenstein Created Woman.* Hammer Films, Great Britain (coproduced with Seven Arts Productions, USA). Directed by Terence Fisher. Produced by Anthony Nelson-Keyes. Screenplay by John Elder (Anthony Hinds). Peter Cushing as Baron Frankenstein, who was brought back to life in time to revive a drowned girl (Susan Denberg) and implant her boyfriend's brain in her skull so that she could avenge her murder.

1967 *Mad Monster Party.* Embassy Pictures, USA. Directed by Jules Bass. Produced by Arthur Rankin, Jr. Screenplay by Len Korobkin and Harvey Kurtzman. Music and lyrics by Maury Laws and Jules Bass. A full-length animated cartoon feature. Boris Karloff supplied the voice of the Frankenstein Monster.

1969 *Frankenstein Must Be Destroyed.* Hammer Films, Great

Britain (released in the USA by Warner Bros.-Seven Arts). Directed by Terence Fisher. Produced by Anthony Nelson-Keyes. Screenplay by Bert Blatt based on a story by Anthony Nelson-Keyes and Bert Blatt. Peter Cushing was Baron Frankenstein, and Freddie Jones was the unfortunate victim of a brain transplant.

1970 *Horror of Frankenstein.* Hammer Films, Great Britain (released in USA by MGM-EMI.) Directed by Jimmy Sangster. Produced by Jimmy Sangster. Screenplay by Jeremy Burnham and Jimmy Sangster. Victor Frankenstein was portrayed by Ralph Bates and the Monster creation by David Prowse.

1971 *Dracula vs. Frankenstein.* Independent-International Films, USA. Directed by Al Adamson. Produced by Al Adamson and Samuel M. Sherman. Screenplay by William Pugsley and Samuel M. Sherman. Zandor Vorkov was Count Dracula and John Bloom the Monster.

1972 *Frankenstein.* Made for TV by Dan Curtis Productions. Directed by Glenn Jordan. Screenplay, Part 1 by Sam Hall, Part 2 by Richard Landau. Robert Foxworth was Dr. Victor Frankenstein, Bo Svenson the Monster.

1973 *Frankenstein: The True Story.* Universal TV, USA. Directed by Jack Smight. Produced by Hunt Stromberg, Jr. The teleplay was by Christopher Isherwood and Don Bachardy. Dr. Frankenstein was played by Leonard Whiting and Michael Sarrazin played his creation.

1974 *Flesh for Frankenstein.* French-Italian (released in the USA as *Andy Warhol's Frankenstein* by Bryanston Pictures). A Carlo Ponti–Andrew Braunsberg–Jean

Pierre Rassam Production. Directed and written by Paul Morrissey. Udo Kier was the Baron and Srdjan Zelenovic was the Monster.

1974 *Frankenstein and the Monster from Hell.* Hammer Films, Great Britain (released in the USA by Paramount). Directed by Terence Fisher. Produced by Roy Skeggs. Screenplay by John Elder (Anthony Hinds). Peter Cushing was Baron Frankenstein. David Prowse played the Monster.

1974 *Young Frankenstein.* 20th Century-Fox, USA. A Gruskoff/Venture/Crossbow/Joner Production. Directed by Mel Brooks. Produced by Michael Gruskoff. Screenplay by Gene Wilder and Mel Brooks. A satire on the Frankenstein legend, with Gene Wilder as Dr. Frederick Frankenstein and Peter Boyle as his Monster.

Bibliography

WORKS BY MARY SHELLEY

History of a Six Weeks' Tour (in collaboration with Shelley):
1817

Frankenstein: or the Modern Prometheus: 1818

Valperga, or, The Life and Adventures of Castruccio, Prince of Lucca: 1823

The Last Man: 1826

The Fortunes of Perkin Warbeck: 1830

Lodore: 1835

Lives in Lardner's *The Cabinet Cyclopaedia (Eminent Literary and Scientific Men of Italy, Spain, and Portugal)*: 1835

Falkner: 1837

Lives in Lardner's *The Cabinet Cyclopaedia (Eminent Literary and Scientific Men of France)*: 1838

Rambles in Germany and Italy in 1840, 1842, and 1843: 1844

"The Choice" (poem) edited by H. B. Forman: 1876

Tales and Stories by M. W. Shelley, collected and edited by R. Garnett: 1891

WORKS BY SHELLEY
EDITED BY MARY SHELLEY

Posthumous Poems of Percy Bysshe Shelley: 1824
The Poetical Works of Percy Bysshe Shelley: 1839
Essays, Letters from Abroad, Translations and Fragments by Percy Bysshe Shelley: 1840

SELECTED BIBLIOGRAPHY

Aldiss, Brian W. *Billion Year Spree: The True History of Science Fiction.* New York: Schocken Books, 1974.

Anobile, Richard J., ed. *Frankenstein.* New York: The Film Classics Library, Avon, 1974.

Blunden, Edmund. *Shelley: A Life Story.* New York: The Viking Press, 1946. (Reprint: Folcroft, Pa.: Folcroft Library Editions.)

Brown, Ford K. *The Life of William Godwin.* New York: E. P. Dutton & Co., 1926. (Reprint: Folcroft, Pa.: Folcroft Library Editions.)

Church, Richard. *Mary Shelley: A Biography.* London: Gerald Howe, Ltd., 1928. (Reprint: Folcroft, Pa.: Folcroft Library Editions.)

Dowden, Edward. *The Life of Percy Bysshe Shelley.* London: Kegan Paul, Trench & Co. Ltd., 1886. (Reprint: Folcroft, Pa.: Folcroft Library Editions.)

Florescu, Radu. *In Search of Frankenstein.* New York: Warner Books, Inc., 1976.

Gerson, Noel Bertram. *Daughter of Earth and Water.* New York: William Morrow, 1973.

Holmes, Richard. *Shelley: The Pursuit.* New York: E. P. Dutton & Co., Inc., 1975.

Jones, Frederick L., ed. *The Letters of Mary W. Shelley.* 2 vols. Norman, Oklahoma: University of Oklahoma Press, 1944.

————. *Mary Shelley's Journal.* Norman, Okla.: University of Oklahoma Press, 1947.

Nitchie, Elizabeth. *Mary Shelley, Author of Frankenstein.* New Brunswick, N.J.: Rutgers University Press, 1953. (Reprint: Westport, Conn.: Greenwood Press, Inc.)

Small, Christopher. *Mary Shelley's Frankenstein: Tracing the Myth.* Pittsburgh, Pa.: University of Pittsburgh Press, 1973.

Spark, Muriel. *Child of Light.* Essex: Tower Bridge Publications, Ltd., 1951. (Reprint: Philadelphia: Richard West.)

————, and Derek Stanford. *My Best Mary: The Selected Letters of Mary Wollstonecraft Shelley.* London: Allan and Wingate, 1953. (Reprint: Philadelphia: Richard West.)

Tomalin, Claire. *The Life and Death of Mary Wollstonecraft.* New York: Harcourt Brace Jovanovich, 1975.

Index

228693 7.95

Harris, Janet

The woman who
created
Frankenstein

DATE			
SEP 29 '82			

© THE BAKER & TAYLOR CO